PRAISE FOR *A SITDOWN WITH THE SOPRANOS*

"In its daring intellectuality, *A Sitdown with the Sopranos* is as gripping as the TV show itself. All of the essays are unfailingly strong and the book's shattering of so many dumb and hurtful conceptions about Italian Americans and their culture will alter American consciousness for good, and for the good."

—Frank Lentricchia, Katherine Everett Gilbert Professor of Literature at Duke University and author of *Lucchesi and The Whale*

"Incisive, funny, and shrewd, this captivating book takes *The Sopranos* seriously as art and a wedge into American cultural troubles. Drawing on the intensity and passion that raise Italian American life to operatic scale, eight sparkling essays show how *The Sopranos* uses America's love affair with the mob family saga as bait for a tragicomic vision of middle class life under siege. Covering everything from gangster chic and male anxiety to canny women and ethnically savvy psychotherapy, this lively, engaging book is essential reading for anyone who cares about popular culture now and the startling use of Italian Americana in its appeal."

—Josephine Gattuso Hendin, Professor of English and Tiro a Segno Professor of Italian American Studies at New York University

"*A Sitdown with the Sopranos* is an excellent collection of essays by eight well-qualified writers who discuss the drama from historical, psychological, feminist, Italian American—and American—perspectives. It all makes for an intelligent and humorous good read."

—Ben Morreale, co-author of *La Storia: Five Centuries of the Italian-American Experience*

Also by Regina Barreca

*They Used to Call Me Snow White . . . But I Drifted: Women's
Strategic Use of Humor*

*Perfect Husbands (& Other Fairy Tales): Demystifying Men,
Marriage, and Romance*

The Penguin Book of Women's Humor, editor

The Signet Book of American Humor, editor

Sweet Revenge: The Wicked Delights of Getting Even

Too Much of a Good Thing is Wonderful

*Don't Tell Mama: The Penguin Book of Italian American
Writing,* editor

*Untamed and Unabashed: Essays on Women and Humor in
British Literature*

A SITDOWN
WITH THE SOPRANOS

Watching Italian American
Culture on TV's
Most Talked-About Series

EDITED BY

REGINA BARRECA

A SITDOWN WITH THE SOPRANOS
Copyright © Regina Barreca, 2002.

First published 2002 by
PALGRAVE MACMILLAN™
175 Fifth Avenue, New York, N.Y. 10010.
Companies and representatives throughout the world.

PALGRAVE MACMILLAN is the global academic imprint of the Palgrave Macmillan division of St. Martin's Press, LLC and of Palgrave Macmillan Ltd. Macmillan® is a registered trademark in the United States, United Kingdom and other countries. Palgrave is a registered trademark in the European Union and other countries.

ISBN 0–312–29528–6 paperback

Library of Congress Cataloging-in-Publication Data
A Sitdown with the Sopranos: watching Italian American culture on TV's most talked-about series / edited by Regina Barreca.
     p.   cm.
  ISBN 0–312–29528–6 (pb)
  1. Sopranos (Television program)   I. Barreca, Regina.
PN1992.77.866 S58   2002
7911.45'72—dc21

                                                                        2002074346

Design by Letra Libre, Inc.

First edition: September 2002
10 9 8 7 6 5 4 3 2 1

Printed in the United States of America

CONTENTS

ACKNOWLEDGEMENTS

When Deborah Gershenowitz from Palgrave sent an email introducing herself and suggesting a book on *The Sopranos,* I was in the rare position of being asked to work on a project I did not have the nerve to suggest myself, so apprehensive was I that an intellectually substantial collection about the show—which I'd adored for two years—would not have been an editor's dream. But since Debbie is herself the editor of one's dreams, I count myself astonishingly fortunate to have been taken under her aegis. The deal was sealed over lunch with Michael Flamini from Palgrave, to whom I am also enormously grateful. Jennifer Stais at the press did a wonderful job throughout the process and worked hard to keep everything on track in New York. In my office at the University of Connecticut, Barbara Campbell, Mara Reisman, and Margaret Mitchell, graduate assistants from heaven, not only kept me on track, but made sure that the volume would be the best thing since *The Sopranos* itself. They are my crew, in the show's parlance, and I trust them with my life. They are honorary Italian Americans—can there be any higher praise? Also honorary members of that club are Brenda Murphy, George Monteiro, and Lee Jacobus, the colleagues who first lured me and my husband, Michael Meyer, into Sopranoland. These four all did a lot of talking about the program without knowing I'd be shoplifting their ideas. Finally, the contributors, souls who were drawn, seduced, and bullied into writing smart and important essays in a big hurry, are of course the ones deserving any and all applause the volume receives. To them, a heartfelt "grazie."

INTRODUCTION

Regina Barreca

"Leave the gun. Take the cannoli."

—The Godfather

A signature phrase of *The Godfather,* the gun/cannoli line is emblematic of what Tony and his family are fitfully trying to accomplish in *The Sopranos:* they want to seize what is best of Italian American culture—the appetites, the passions, the affections, the humor—while leaving behind on the table the bitterness, the alienation, the crime, and the violence.

Anybody have a problem with that? If *The Sopranos* is not moving ahead as expeditiously as we Italian Americans might like on the "cannoli" angle of this agenda, it has nevertheless become self-evident that the show is a lightning-rod for some of the most significant issues in contemporary American culture. That, in part, is why this book exists.

So why are all the contributors to this book of Italian American descent? Ask it another way: Why should Italian Americans get dealt a favorable hand when sitting down with the Sopranos? Why make the discussion ethnic-specific? Why not see *The Sopranos* as the last frontier of the universally appealing story where all viewers criticize and appreciate with equally insightful and informed responses? A charming thought, but misleading.

In any audience watching a powerful story, you will find those who laugh and those who weep. Even if we laugh or weep at the same time, however, it does not necessarily follow that we are all laughing or weeping at precisely the same things. Our heritage and our parochialism inform our responses as viewers (for that matter, so does class, gender, sexual orientation, predilections in music, and taste in clothes—remember how much Tony Soprano hates the jacket given to him by Richie Aprile?). What is significant is the fact that you have to earn the membership to an inside group: you must be initiated. Ethnicity works the same way. Would you tell a joke about a Dubliner if you were at an Irish pub—and you weren't Irish? Would you make an Amos and Andy joke if you were on stage at the Apollo Theater? Would you tell an Italian joke at a Sons of Italy meeting if you weren't Italian? You would know better than to assume that you understood fully what it was like to be in that group if you were dealing with members of that group, right?

And so it is of particular importance to place Italian American voices at the center of a discussion of *The Sopranos,* because the series has been attacked from within and from outside the Italian American community as undignified and biased. Without being defined as such, the study of *The Sopranos* has become the study of contemporary culture's vision of Italian Americans. Because of this, eight leading Italian American scholars, writers, critics, journalists, theorists, and professors have gathered in this volume to consider the HBO television series.

Of course Italian Americans want to discuss *The Sopranos.* Let's face it—everybody wants to discuss *The Sopranos.* The show has captured our collective imagination because while it is certainly set in an Italian American world, it is not simply or even mostly about issues understood or experienced only by Italian Americans. To reduce *The Sopranos* to being a story about violent Italian Americans is like saying that *Hamlet* is a story about moody Danes. The people who make this argument are not entirely incorrect, but they sure are missing the main point.

George Anastasia explains this beautifully in his essay "If Shakespeare Were Alive Today, He'd Be Writing for *The Sopranos.*" Anger, violence, and alienation are what propel the plot of the show—and keep the audience enthralled. Anastasia, a reporter for the *Philadelphia Inquirer,* reminds us that *The Sopranos* is first and foremost a story. Organized crime is the backdrop. It's the vehicle used to drive the narrative. Tony Soprano is Everyman. He has problems. He struggles, sometimes in unusual ways, to deal with them. Sometimes he succeeds. Sometimes he fails. Millions of viewers tune in each week because they care what happens. That's why the drama works.

King Lear offered the same kind of attraction. You think you've got problems, look at this guy. And he's king of England, for crying out loud. If it's *Mister Lear* the play closes in a week.

"If the stereotype of an Italian American is someone who wants to grab life with both hands, someone who loves to eat good food, loves to spend hours with his extended family, someone who's not afraid to show emotions, I can live with that," Anastasia shrugs. "And if that character is a mobster or a detective or a sports writer, what's the difference? It's about who they are, not what they do."

It is not the crime family but the struggle for intimacy, affection, humor, and success on the part of the extended domestic family that keeps the series at the forefront of contemporary popular culture. It is worth noting that Tony, ruler of New Jersey, and Hamlet, Prince of Denmark, are indeed alike. Both are profoundly introspective and prone to self-doubt, intimidated by formidable mothers, worried about public roles, concerned about treacherous uncles, and irresolute in matters of the heart. They have their attendant lords: Paulie and Pussy, right alongside Rosencrantz and Guildenstern, are concerned with the specter of the boss's dead father. The worlds inhabited by Tony and Hamlet appear to them as stale, flat, and unprofitable (or, as Tony puts it, "I'm losing my mind here"). While Hamlet muses that "There is providence in the fall of a sparrow," Tony wonders about destiny and the flight of his ducks ("You think that everything that happens is preordained?" asks Tony's therapist, Dr. Melfi, knowing the answer is "yes"). There is method to their madness.

And their madness is dealt with directly. "*The Sopranos* puts the entirety of Italian American culture on the couch," argues Michael Flamini, a New York writer and editor who trained in clinical psychology. In order to come to a full understanding of their culture, he suggests, Italian Americans must "face the horror and ugliness of Mob history, our Italian American Id." Only then will they be able to say to other Americans, "Yes, that's part of my world, but not all of it. Get over it."—and move on.

As Americans, we have always enjoyed the exploits of the exciting out-sider: bounty hunters, spies, call girls, private detectives, and outlaws intrigue us. Mobsters are one of the primary mythopoeic creations of the twentieth- and twenty-first centuries: they capture our collective imagination as effi-ciently as they move hot DVD players. We dream about them; we make movies about them; they shock us by revealing parts of ourselves we would like to deny. "*The Sopranos* succeeds by taking what is 'normal' and exagger-ating it; it draws attention to the fault lines in family and community life," argues Jay Parini, novelist, poet, and professor of English at Middlebury Col-lege, "and it makes overt what is usually covert. It plays with stereotypes, winking at us as it does so, treading a line between realism and fantasy."

The outsider's hunger for acceptance often is met with hostility, preju-dice, and hypocrisy. And so, unable to blend into the crowd, their deviance increasingly becomes their definition. This is the story of the characters in *The Sopranos*. Since these outsiders can't join those who are in control of in-stitutionalized power, they beat them. And beat them at their own game. Part of what bothers Tony Soprano about "them" is the fact that those who hold the winning hand never have played fairly. "When they let the Italians in," Tony insists, "they didn't do it to save us from poverty but because they needed us . . . to build their cities, dig their subways, to make them richer, the Carnegies and the Rockefellers—they needed worker bees and there we were. But some of us didn't want to swarm around their hive and lose who we were. We wanted to stay Italian and preserve the things that meant some-thing to us . . . honor and family and loyalty." Then he adds after a brief pause, "And some of us wanted a piece of the action." Although the policies, principles, and philosophies of those who have historically dominated Amer-ican culture are advertised as righteous, fair, and accessible to the public, Tony is not blind to the hypocrisy of the dominant system. Like Michael Corleone, who quips that Italian Americans must "learn from the philan-thropists like the Rockefellers: first you rob everybody, then you give to the poor," Tony understands that to be permitted into the halls of power, he'll have to break in through the windows—it is unlikely that he will be admit-ted through the front door.

After all, Tony is not your ordinary New Jersey businessman (although, as his therapist Dr. Melfi tells him, "in spite of everything, you're a very con-ventional man"). A mobster involved in racketeering, illegal gambling, prostitution, loansharking, and other nefarious activities too numerous to mention, his "legit" job isn't exactly ideal, either—not if we're coming from a politically correct standpoint. This fortyish father of two reports daily to a strip club called The Bada Bing. Ensconced in the back room with his cronies, Tony spends most of his time organizing the crime family. Meanwhile girls wearing g-strings undulate on a stage in the front of the bar. (Interestingly enough, for all the sexual presence they command, these girls might as well be members of a typing pool.) Yet Tony and his crew live pretty well, send their children to private high schools and Ivy League universities, and are active in the church. The very presence of the Sopranos in the upper-middle-class world of a metropolitan suburb is flung down like a gauntlet, offering a challenge to the system that would confine these Italian Americans to the realm of the appropriately disenfranchised. With their reputations, how can they be accepted?

Characters in *The Sopranos* are unable to divorce themselves from their reputations—or their representations. They are haunted by the romantic qualities they believe existed in the "golden days" of Johnny Boy Soprano's reign even as they reject the old ways. (Johnny Boy was Tony's father; a talent for working in organized crime appears to run in families, like blue blood.) Nostalgic for the wise-guy Eden they believe existed in a world before RICO, Tony's crew manufactures a fanciful legacy made up of snippets from movies with Jimmy Cagney and Al Pacino, thereby creating a world that never existed—and yet cannot be forgotten. In other words, almost everything about *The Sopranos* makes it sound profoundly offensive to Italian Americans.

Some Italian American groups have declared the program ruinous to the image of Americans of Italian descent, an insulting and viciously misrepresentative depiction of an aberrant world with which the overwhelming majority of Italian Americans have no experience. In fact, *The Sopranos* grapples with the suggestion that Italian Americans will be pushed further away from the mainstream by depictions of mobsters who happen to be Italian. Undercutting the weight of the argument, however, is the fact that it is made repeatedly within the framework of the program by psychiatrist Jennifer Melfi's ex-husband Richard. The argument is defanged by putting it in the mouth of a bitter, unsympathetic man given to pronouncements such as "I'm so fed up with people thinking I'm a thug because my name ends in a vowel." Richard sees the world through a self-serving and myopic lens, always arriving at the same conclusion: Italian Americans are victims of prejudice. (Ironically enough, he and Tony Soprano would see eye-to-eye on this matter.) Several times Dr. Melfi tries to kid her ex-husband out of his sanctimonious refusal to see anything aside from his own dogmatic position. ("Condescend to me, Richard, it gets me so hot . . .") "Your Calabrese is showing," she chides him during another heated discussion of the issue, and later goes on to declare that she's amazed that with the world in as much trouble as it is, "You devote your energies to the protection of the dignity of Connie Francis." Dr. Melfi's ex-husband can and does continue to trot out convincing statistics with the best of them: "Italians Against Discrimination did a study, and at its height the Mafia in this country had less than 5,000 members. And yet that tiny insignificant fraction casts such a dark shadow over 20 million hard-working Americans." Richard means well in his sensitivity to Italian American stereotyping. He sees himself as a voice of conscience, a voice crying out in the wilderness of New Jersey, no less.

But do-gooders end badly in *The Sopranos;* not that they are always murdered, but they are mocked. Whether they are coaches, priests, lawyers, fundraising officials from Columbia University, school psychologists, or defenders of the dignity of Connie Francis, busybodies of all stripes are portrayed as smug, foolish, and manipulative at best. *The Sopranos* systematically undercuts self-awarded moral authority by sardonically usurping its very voice. Toward the end of the episode in which Dr. Jennifer Melfi is raped, for example, she realizes that her ex-husband Richard is distracted from his genuine concern for her by his own worry that the man who raped her appears to have an Italian surname. She hisses at him: "Are you so ashamed of your background that any misdeed by an Italian damages your self-esteem?" Within this line lies curled an embryonic counterargument to those who vilify the show.

"Like God or Santa Claus," Sandra M. Gilbert argues, the creator of *The Sopranos* anticipates viewers' responses to the show, including the complaints that are likely to be made about the portrayal of Italian Americans as gangsters, "even while building tough answers into the heart of the debate." Gilbert, professor of English at the University of California, Davis, points out that the show undermines the "anti-Media Mafia" argument by placing it "in the mouth" of Richard, "the least sympathetic character at the table," while attributing the counter-position ("at this point in our cultural history,

Mob movies are classic American cinema") to the earnest undergraduate son, Jason.

If Gilbert makes the argument that the language of the show perfectly captures and echoes certain cultural positions that inform the critical responses to *The Sopranos,* Jay Parini contends that the same "perfect pitch" is at work in the depiction of the attitudes of the characters themselves. Their speech, their body language, their expressions "all seem real," according to Parini; all are "brilliantly choreographed." This carefully produced sense of authenticity charges even the most intimate moments of the show.

Tony and his families question implicitly and explicitly much that is sanctified in contemporary American culture. They have tried to keep up with the times, attempted to travel routes of self-discovery and sensitivity. Not that these routes have inevitably led to satisfactory ends. As Tony complains, "Uncle Junior and I, we had our problems with the business. But I never should have razzed him about eating pussy. This whole war could have been averted. Cunnilingus and psychiatry brought us to this." Both cunnilingus and psychiatry would have been considered unmanly in an earlier generation. Fred Gardaphé, scholar of Italian American culture and head of the American and Italian/American Studies Programs at SUNY Stonybrook, argues that "The American man is changing; this is what *The Sopranos* is telling us. There is only one way I know by which a man can be made into a soprano; metaphorically this is what is happening to Tony Soprano, who happens to be a gangster in a time in which traditional notions of manhood are reeling. . . . Like many male baby boomers in the throes of middle age, Tony is trying to figure out who he is and why he does what he does. . . . [H]e begins to question the traditional order of things and this leads him to question his role as a husband, a father, a son, and a gangster."

E. Anthony Rotundo, Instructor of History and Social Sciences at Phillips Academy and author of *American Manhood: Transformations in Masculinity from the Revolution to the Modern Era,* agrees: "For the vast majority of Italian American men who live in the legitimate mainstream, their gangster brethren are like the proverbial train-wreck—they can't help but look." These ordinary, mainstream men, Rotundo argues, have also made choices, even if they are less obvious than the ones made by men like Tony Soprano. Such men—those who have chosen to play by the rules—"can look at mobsters and see people they may have known living out the choices that they—living a 'straight' life—chose not to make." Rotundo's essay also illustrates the point that *The Sopranos* "shows us a variety of Italian American men outside the mob—Father Phil and Dr. Cusamano and (especially and respectfully) Artie Bucco. Finally, *The Sopranos* gives us values such as loyalty, rootedness, and interdependence—values that have provided a foundation for Italian American manhood." Rotundo contends that "Part of Tony's humanity—and part of his tragedy—is that he knows America (whatever its common pieties) is hostile to those values." Tony "believes in his soul that those values—and not gunplay—are what Italian American men could have brought to American culture."

And the vicissitudes of American culture still baffle characters on *The Sopranos*. When Paulie Walnuts, the most violent of Tony's associates, goes to his first Starbucks-style coffee shop, he cannot understand why his compatriots missed out on the racket to sell overpriced coffee and cake, those very staples of Italian American existence. Paulie sees the theft of the Italian espresso bar as a great con pulled by a so-called legitimate business. He struggles with a sense of what another character dismisses as "the rape of the culture," wondering inwardly, "why didn't we do this, put this in place?" When Paulie steals an espresso maker, it is clear that he has a desire for reparations, not for appliances. There is a palpable sense of combined frustration and regret that Italians didn't consider this avenue to "legit" wealth.

Similarly, when Tony's nephew Christopher is betrayed by a young woman from a Hollywood studio who seduces him both sexually and intellectually by encouraging him to give her his film script—from which she and a friend then lift several key scenes—Christopher is amazed by her lack of integrity. "Oh, you're good," he says, as she unflinchingly looks him in the eyes. "Fucking Walnuts don't lie as good as you." However adept any of the Sopranos become at subverting the system, the system—ubiquitous, crooked, corrupt, iniquitous, and in control—remains relentlessly intact.

The ordinary dominant world outside the world of the family appears populated by smug and pious fools who long to see anyone who enjoys life appropriately punished; they seem not to mind what pleasures the characters have had in the past, as long as they are made miserable at the finish. Presumably the argument runs something like this: If the outsiders do not pay and keep paying, how are all the insiders going to get satisfaction out of watching them suffer? And then what would happen to the pride of being an insider? What's the payoff for being good if the wicked do not perish—or at least get locked up?

Moral and ethical battlefields are the landscapes of this series. In her essay on *The Sopranos* and religion, historian Carla Gardina Pestana regards the depiction of the spiritual conflicts of its characters, religious or otherwise, in fairly authentic terms. "Many characters, Tony among them, feel a fierce pride in their Italian heritage and its Roman Catholicism." She continues, "The commitment to continuing the family's association with the Catholic Church across the generations—even among those with tortured or attenuated personal relationships to the Church—is quite realistic. The characters, for all their egregious acts, are rendered sympathetically. This portrayal of likable murderers is part of what makes the show so provocative and troubling. But by humanizing these people in a way that has not been done in any treatment of the Mafia in the popular media to date, we can also appreciate their personal struggles."

Although it was applauded by television critics from its first episode, *The Sopranos* didn't need critical praise to become the hit of HBO during its first season. It sold itself through word of mouth, and the word was good along every avenue of American life. There is substantial evidence that *The Sopranos* has a surprising resonance in American and, most recently, European culture. Sandra Gilbert addresses this topic directly— "why . . . 'is Italian-American (and Italian) organized crime such a mainstay of American pop culture?'" She argues that, ultimately, the responses to the show fall into three categories: "*The Sopranos R Us*," "*The Sopranos R Art*," and "*The Sopranos R Postmodern Art*." The first implies a sense of identification, whether real or wishful; the second places the show within a certain literary tradition, invoking the likes of Balzac and Zola; and the third—and the most academic—attributes to *The Sopranos* a theoretically complex blend of "allusiveness, irony, and self-reflexiveness."

But of course *The Sopranos* need not only be interpreted as a hotbed of deconstructive intellectualism. In fact, it has been tricky to do a book about a television series in which the representative connubial relationship can be summed up by the line, "When you're married, you'll understand the importance of fresh produce"; where a near-death experience for one of the characters leads to an ethnic-specific vision of hell (after being shot, Christopher sees "our hell: an Irish bar where it's St. Patrick's every day—for ever. Playing dice and the Irish winning every roll"); and where the act of reading itself is not exactly celebrated but is instead regarded as soporific (when Dr. Melfi recommends a book to Tony he sheepishly admits "I read, I go right out").

It's been tricky to do a book about complex characters too often reduced, by critics and viewers alike, to mere caricature. Neither Tony Soprano, nor even the most sketchily presented member of his family, is simply a caricature. Only a calculated misreading of *The Sopranos* can make him one. Tony is one of television's most dauntless inventions because David Chase, the show's creator, writer, and director, demands that we forgo our desire to approve of the hero.

That is one of the reasons why this book, written by Italians, is not only for Italians. Complicated issues of real importance have been spotlighted by this series: nothing less than the very notion of the hyphenated ethnic experience is being invoked by Chase's "monster" (as Tony once refers to himself). But the Italian American experience being spotlighted here is a reflection of all the other versions of itself. And the spotlight turns the mirror into a prism: the Jewish experience in America, the Irish experience in America, the Polish experience in America, the Hispanic experience in America, and even in some ways the African American experience in America are all illuminated. *The Sopranos* is about the human experience—about all of us, about the struggle to find a safe place, sanctuaries of the heart and mind and conscience, for ourselves and those we love.

And it's also a terrific television show.

LIFE WITH (GOD)FATHER

Sandra M. Gilbert

O Mafiosi,
bad uncles of the barren
cliffs of Sicily—was it only you
that they transported in barrels
like pure olive oil
across the Atlantic?

—Sandra M. Gilbert, *"Mafioso"*

Ihave to admit that I'm more than a little bemused by my own willingness not just to *watch* a sitcom (if that's what it is) about an Italian American gangster clan called *The Sopranos* but even to write an essay about their doings and misdoings. Indeed, I'm only inditing such a piece because the editor of this volume made me an offer I couldn't refuse—couldn't refuse once I realized it would give me a chance to meditate on a subject that's long troubled me: the vexing representations of "my" people in all too many media megahits.

For I should say at once that I'm a person who runs screaming from the room if anyone dares to put *The Godfather I, II,* or *III* in the VCR. True, I saw the first work in the series, the primordial *Godfather* as it were, almost as soon as it came out, and I remember priding myself on the steeliness with which I withstood repellent scenes over which some critics expressed shock and horror (for instance, the infamous episode of the horse's head). But something happened between my first encounter with Marlon Brando's jowly, whispery Don Corleone and the development of commercial home video, something about my sense of what it meant and means to me to be an Italian American. And for decades now that *something* has led me to shrink in fear and loathing from any further acquaintance with Corleone and his misbegotten "family."

What makes my recalcitrance—to understate the feeling—especially odd is the fact that my own, real-life family has never shared my distaste for Coppola's masterworks; rather, they've always considered my violent anti-*Godfather*ness a lamentable eccentricity. My Sicilian-born mother, who should after all have been especially sensitive to the movie's unpleasant representations of compatriots, long professed to admire, indeed, to love the three movies—and never in fact considered that they had any significant relationship to her own life. As for those members of my inner circle most expert in film history and theory—my late husband, a video collector and movie connoisseur, and our son, also one of the *cognoscenti*—both made many (fruitless) efforts to help me "appreciate" Coppola's artfulness. Many a time and oft, as I remember all too well, they'd sit me down in front of the VCR with snacks, drinks, and running commentaries on camera angles, "texture," acting styles, et cetera. And indeed when they first began their well-meant attempts at educating me in the fine points of what they claimed were cinematic classics, I'd usually manage to last twenty or thirty minutes in front of the glimmering screen. Then, suddenly, the *something* would happen and I'd jump up, spilling my soda or dumping my popcorn on the coffee table, and run screaming, or at any rate infuriated, from the room.

Eventually, I just ran screaming from the room if I heard the whisper of Don Corleone's voice or the telltale beat of the tarantella. Ditto the Mafioso word "family."

For the *something* had to do with my own family, and more particularly with the definitions and redefinitions of familial ethnicity that changed so many people's ways of looking at the cultural landscape sometime toward the end of the 1970s. That was the era, remember, when a number of us who weren't WASP males discovered that we'd been living all along (and mostly without noticing anything problematic) in a sexist,

racist, Eurocentric—indeed *Anglo*centric—society, and that therefore slices
of the cultural pie weren't exactly divided equally. For me as a budding
feminist critic this meant learning to reimagine literary texts all over again
and, in doing so, coming to terms with the fact that for much of my life I'd
been, as the American studies and women's studies scholar Judith Fetterley
once put it, "identifying *against*" myself—identifying, for example, with
Twain's Huck Finn, the roguish boy hero, while laughing at Emmeline
Grangerford, the stupid sentimental would-be "poetess"; identifying with
Dickens's Pip while scorning mad Miss Havisham and her twisted pro-
tegee, the proud beauty Estella.[1] All too often, in other words, I was discovering that a female incarnation of foolishness, madness, or wickedness
occupied the place in the text where I myself, as a woman and an aspiring
poet, might have played a part in whatever story I was reading. Thus, as I
came to realize, if I had wanted to imagine myself as heroic or creative
throughout my childhood and young adulthood I'd usually have had to
cast myself as a male.

And a WASP male: certainly not an Italian American! What images, after
all, had my culture shown me of the very people who'd given my father his
patronymic name (Mortola), my mother hers (Caruso), and me my genes?
Chico Marx portraying a stereotypical organ grinder, with his squealing instru-
ment, silly monkey, and "Dago" accent? The pathetic immigrants of Frank
Capra's *It's a Wonderful Life*, living in squalor among goats and chickens?

The burgeoning group- and self-awarenesses that were fostered by the
so-called Second Wave of feminism and were to issue in what we today call
"identity politics" cast me into gloom. Just as I suddenly understood that
along with countless other women I'd been the recipient of a rain of cultural
messages excluding me from imaginative authority, so too I became aware
that as an Italian American I'd been relegated to a somewhat comic, perhaps
even grotesque underclass.

But wait, maybe that underclass wasn't just *comic;* maybe it was sinister,
too. Of course like any other American I knew there were bad, gangland Italians. I'd heard the word "Mafia" or anyway read it in newspapers. But perhaps in fact it wasn't until I saw *The Godfather* that I made a connection
between a Sicilian American family like my mother's large and lively tribe,
and wicked headliners like Frank Costello and Lucky Luciano, the Murder,
Inc., bosses of the New York underworld.

Was it precisely the persuasive Italian Americanness (what some scholars in the new field of Italian American Studies might call the "*Italianita*") so vividly dramatized in *The Godfather* that surfaced the *something* I found so infuriating? Was it the *plausibility* of these people—their unnervingly familiar ways of dancing, laughing, dressing, eating, and drinking—that so distressed me? I think it must have been, for I remember it was around the time Coppola's movie first came out that I was seized by the blazing epiphany that I recorded in "Mafioso," the poem that I've somewhat narcissistically used as an epigraph here.

What I had to say in this poem, as I recall, was so uncomfortable that I had to shield myself from its nastiness by trying to make the whole sickening problem funny. And to this day "Mafioso" gets a lot of laughs when I launch into it at readings:

> Frank Costello eating spaghetti in a cell at San Quentin,
> Lucky Luciano mixing up a mess of bullets and
>   calling for parmesan cheese,
> Al Capone baking a sawed-off shotgun into a
>   huge lasagna—
> are you my uncles, my
>   only uncles?

But as I was ultimately forced to declare in the poem itself, I had by now learned that the situation of the Italian American immigrant community was deeply *un*funny. It wasn't, after all, only the bad, Mafioso "uncles of the barren/cliffs of Sicily" who had been "transported" like "pure olive oil/across the Atlantic"! It wasn't only they

> who got out at Ellis Island with
> black scarves on [their] heads and cheap cigars
> and no English and a dozen children. . . .

On the contrary, it was my mother's mother the midwife, and her older brothers the *socialisti* rebels, and her father the tailor, and my other uncles the pharmacy students, one of whom recited Virgil as he washed the dishes and another of whom wrote poetry and studied Latin at City College until he went mad—it was *they* and many others like them who had been "transported" into a scary, chilly New World where

> No carts were waiting, gallant with paint,
> no little donkeys plumed like the dreams of peacocks.
> Only the evil eyes of a thousand buildings
> stared across at the echoing debarkation center,
> making it seem so much smaller than a piazza,
>
> only a half dozen Puritan millionaires stood on the wharf,
> in the wind colder than the impossible snows of the Abruzzi,
> ready with country clubs and dynamos
>
> to grind the organs out of you.

Nor did my Sicilian grandparents, uncles, aunts, and cousins respond with operatic rage to the WASP New World that held them, so far as I can tell, in considerable contempt. I'm not sure what they knew of the Mafia in the old life they'd left behind, but to my knowledge they learned little about American gangland doings after they settled in Brooklyn.

One of the brothers, yes, "went bad," got involved in petty crimes, was mysteriously deported, and ended up scraping together a hand-to-mouth living in Rome, where various aunts regularly sent him care packages of old sweaters, suits, and shoes, as if he were a one-man Goodwill recipient. But as for the others, all of them—the parents, the six remaining brothers, the two sisters, and their geometrically multiplying children—were too busy for major misbehavior: too busy learning English, delivering babies, tailoring suits, and scrambling, painfully but passionately, up the educational ladder.

Whichever Italian Americans were offing each other in mobster killings, buying and selling *paesan* crooners, and getting rich in violent get-rich-quick schemes, those Italian Americans weren't *my* Sicilian-born relatives, most of whom studied their English or Latin or night-school "citizenship" primers in cramped floor-through walk-ups not far from the Williamsburg Bridge, on the narrow side streets off Bushwick Avenue, where, night and day, the El used to rage back and forth between Manhattan and Brooklyn.

And, putting aside the mythic Corleone family, what about the forebears of the Sopranos? Did they land on the same icy shore where my Caruso grandparents got off the boat? Considering that they must have, what's the secret of their success—or do I mean their *un*success, their spectacular (and from the perspective of their fans, utterly charismatic) inability to adapt to such generally accepted social norms as "Thou shalt not kill?"

I'm not, of course, the first Italian American commentator to be exasperated by the bizarre American hang-up on what we might call Media Mafiosi. As the third season of *The Sopranos* got underway in 2001, the Illinois-based American Italian Defense Association filed a lawsuit against HBO, claiming that the series "suggests that criminality is in the blood or in the genes of Italian-Americans, and that Italians as early immigrants to this country had little opportunity other than to turn to crime."[2] But writing in *The Nation* a year earlier, the journalist George de Stefano had already noted the inclination of numerous Italian Americans to be, at the very least, irked by "the seemingly endless stream of Mafia movies and TV shows." In January 2000, he reminded readers, "a coalition of seven Italian-American organizations issued a joint statement condemning *The Sopranos* for 'defaming and assassinating the cultural character' of Americans of Italian descent." But why, after all, he went on to wonder, "is Italian-American (and Italian) organized crime such a mainstay of American pop culture"?[3]

Focusing on *The Sopranos,* an array of *non*–Italian American video pundits—from online groupies to high-minded *New York Times* reviewers to hyper-theoretical postmodern academics—have come up with a dizzying range of answers to de Stefano's important question, most of which can ultimately be placed in one or another of the following three categories:

1. The simplest but perhaps most heartfelt responses fall under the rubric *The Sopranos R Us.* (And even if we don't think they R, we wish they were.) This is a view perhaps best exemplified by the enraptured musings of Joyce Millman on salon.com. "You don't have to be Italian for *The Sopranos* to hit home," enthuses Millman, just as, in her opinion, "You don't have to be Italian to feel like one of *la famiglia* watching *The Godfather*." Indeed, she adds, the "Sopranos are no more dysfunctional than any other upper-middle class subur-

ban brood"—i.e., *The Sopranos R Us.* But even when they aren't, we wish they were: "in one enviable way," Millman burbles, "they may be *less* dysfunctional—at least this family sits down to eat dinner together every night."

And what dinners the Sopranos sit down to! Judging from Millman's fervor, Carmela's kitchen in suburban New Jersey really explains why They ought to *be* Us (or maybe We ought to be Them). The "food—my God, the food!," swoons Millman; "I mean, doesn't your mouth water when Carmela takes another steaming dish of baked rigatoni out of the oven, or Tony twirls his spaghetti around a meatball as big as his fist?" In sum, she concludes,

> "The Sopranos" woos third and fourth generation Americans—grown beyond our ancestors' ethnic identities, hometown loyalties and economic classes—with what we crave most: roots. You watch "The Sopranos" and it stirs some deep-down tribal memory. You feel like you know this family, these people with their big emotions and their messy relationships and their ties that bind, and in some strange way, you feel like you're home.[4]

2. A slightly more complex (but equally heartfelt) set of responses to the (mis)adventures of Tony S. & Co. might be labeled *The Sopranos R Art.* (You thought this was a run-of-the-mill soap opera *cum* gangster movie blend? Wise up; reread your Zola, your Balzac, your Proust.)

In this vein, Caryn James, the often incisive and insightful TV reviewer for *The New York Times,* weighs in with a meditation rather more august than Millman's, magisterially proclaiming that the HBO series "lives at the juncture where pop culture and high art meet," and adding that

> Like Zola's Rougon-Macquart series or Balzac's "Comedie Humaine," *The Sopranos* defines a particular culture (suburban New Jersey at the turn of the century) but using complex individuals. So what if Tony is not a prostitute out of Balzac but a mobster out of David Chase's imagination? His outlaw status offers a way of assessing mainstream society in all its savagery and hypocrisy, even while the series creates a unique family history.

To be sure, James is aware that some constituencies might take offense at the stereotyping dynamics of "David Chase's imagination." "Mr. Chase has been the target of *wrong-headed* complaints [emphasis added] that the series maligns Italian-Americans," she concedes. Yet in his wisdom, she argues, the show's auteur "casually illuminates how true bias manifests itself: the F.B.I. calls the Sopranos' house 'the sausage factory,'" failing to understand that when "they plant their wire [they'll] hear nothing more revealing than Carmela telling her husband, 'What you need is more roughage overall in your diet.'"[5] (Perhaps, then, *The Sopranos R Art* because Tony Soprano is such a "complex individual" that he doesn't spend a whole lot of time discussing his professional, rather than personal, "Waste Management Business" in that scrumptious kitchen of which Millman is so fond.)

3. *The Sopranos R Postmodern Art.* Critics offering responses that fall into this category mostly and not surprisingly tend to be academic intellectuals and/or their "real world" counterparts. And at least in part their views of the show chime with those proffered by commentators whom I've grouped into my first two categories. In other words, yes, theorists of postmodernity would agree that *The Sopranos R Us* because after all the *famiglia* of (twenty-first-century American) "man" is fierce, confusing, and hungry for rigatoni. And yes, these theorists would also agree that *The Sopranos R Art* because after all what is "art"? Isn't it anyway everything or nothing, "pop culture" *plus* "elite creation"? But most significantly, these thinkers would add that *The Sopranos R Postmodern Art* precisely because their auteur has not only seen *The Godfather* movies (along with dozens of others) besides reading Balzac, Zola, etc.; he and his associates cannily *clue us in* to all they've seen and read through the deft displays of "intertextuality," allusiveness, irony, and self-reflexiveness with which they lace every episode of their show.

A typical proponent of this *Sopranos as Postmodern Art* thesis is David Lavery, a Professor of English at Middle Tennessee State University and the author of an online meditation called "Coming Heavy," which bears as subtitle the daunting admonition "To really 'make it' as a *Sopranos* watcher, come with your full breadth of cultural references or don't come at all."[6] Notes Lavery, the "predominance of the 'already said,' as Umberto Eco once observed, is, after all, one of postmodernism's signatures" (and it doesn't hurt this critic that Eco has "already said" what he, Lavery, wants to say). Defining *The Sopranos* as a "continuing gangster series—fully, self-consciously, even hyper-consciously, mobbed-up—hybridized in the age of re-combinant TV with a family drama," Lavery notes that the show's "intertextuality reveals much about its genre," tracks down a host of allusions to precursor films or texts, and attempts a quasi-structuralist narratological analysis of Chase's work through a table featuring side-by-side summaries of "Robert Warshow's classic comparison of the gangster film and the western [as first] published in *Film Theory and Criticism* (Oxford, 1992)."

Well. When confronted with such an overwhelming array of emotional and intellectual defenses—*The Sopranos R Us, The Sopranos R Art, The Sopranos R Postmodern Art*—what is one poor, embattled, Italian American televiewer to do? Her problem, indeed, becomes especially complicated because in his brilliantly postmodern way auteur David Chase (né De Cesare, as de Stefano slyly informs us) even acknowledges the anxieties of *paesan* viewers. In the exceptionally self-reflexive and allusive episode entitled "The Legend of Tennessee Moltisanti," the *Sopranos* script features hopelessly untalented neophyte bad guy Christopher Moltisanti struggling to write—what else?—a *script,* and of course it's a *gangster* script not merely because gangland life is just about the only thing Christopher understands but also because, as he eagerly explains to his long-suffering girlfriend Adriana, *"Mob stories are always hot."* Then, built into the center of this episode as if to confirm that besides being "always hot," *"Mob stories are always about Italian Americans,"* comes a token dinnertime debate about the media tendency to conflate the Mob, the Mafia, and the American citizen of Italian descent.

This time the scrumptious (of course Italian) food is being dished out not by Carmela Soprano but by shrink Dr. Jennifer Melfi's kindly gray-haired mama, who's serving pasta to her grandson, her husband, her daughter, and her daughter's ex-husband when grandson Jason's use of the derogatory word "ginzo" precipitates a heated discussion of the ways in which "scum" like Melfi's nameless gangland patient give Italian Americans a "bad image."

Richard (Melfi's ex): Ask any American to describe an Italian-American in this country, invariably he's gonna reference *The Godfather, Goodfellas.*

Jason: Good movies.

Richard: And the rest are gonna mention pizza.

Jason: Good movies to eat pizza by.

Richard: Stop it, Jason.

Jennifer: I never said he [Tony] was in the Mafia.

Richard: Why do you think we're never gonna see an Italian president?

Jennifer: Oh, and that's my patient's fault. I realize that you're very involved in the anti-defamation lobby. So go after Hollywood, if you feel you absolutely have to. But leave my patient alone.

Richard: It's a synergy. News items and the constant portrayal of Italian-Americans as gangsters.

Jason: Wasn't the Italian anti-def deal started by Joe Colombo? A mobster?

Richard: Italians Against Discrimination did a study, and at its height the Mafia in this country had less than 5,000 members. And yet that tiny insignificant fraction casts such a dark shadow over 20 million hard-working Americans.

Jason: Dad, at this point in our cultural history, mob movies are classic American cinema. Like westerns.

And there it is! Like God or Santa Claus, the ultra-cool creator of *The Sopranos* always already anticipates our responses: he sees us when we're sleeping, knows when we're awake, and most important predicts the complaints *some* of us may level against shows like his ("the constant portrayal of Italian-Americans as gangsters" means we may "never see an Italian president") even while building tough answers into the heart of the debate ("the Italian anti-def deal" was itself started by a mobster but in any case "mob movies are classic American cinema"). More telling still, he deftly places the most serious part of the anti-Media-Mafia argument in the mouth of the least sympathetic character at the table—Richard, the sourpuss ex, himself a shrink, whose professional advice to his former wife about her unsavory patient ("Just refer him to another doctor") prompts her vehement "Now I remember why we got divorced." Just as telling, too, he gives the high-toned clincher ("at this point in our cultural history, mob movies are classic American cinema") to Jason, the earnest undergrad, whose innocence is matched by the skill with which he mediates between his fretful parents.

Clearly, judging from judicious Jason's reaction to his dad's protests, Chase/De Cesare's petulant *paesani* aren't going to get much support from the next generation. For those of us who don't cotton to the ways in which, as Manny Alfano, chairman of the Italian American AntiBias Committee puts it, "almost ALL of the fictional Italo American characters on TV and in movies [are portrayed as] dimwits, bimbos, bums, or buffoons if not criminals," maybe there's only one solution: in the words of yet another onscreen caricature of Italian Americans-as-mobsters, *Analyze This.*[7]

Let's begin with Joyce Millman's interesting assertions that "You don't have to be Italian for *The Sopranos* to hit home," and "You don't have to be Italian to feel like one of *la famiglia* watching *The Godfather.*" As an Italian American, I have to say that I'm bemused (to put it mildly) by these remarks. Is Millman implying that *The Sopranos* ought to "hit home" for me in some special way because the show reflects my ethnic "heritage"? Is she arguing that when I watch *The Godfather* I should inevitably be reminded of my own *famiglia*? If so, I'd have to say she's got her claims quite wrong.

In one sense, though, Millman's misapprehension of me-as-representative-Italian American is noteworthy: It does reveal something significant about the writer herself and also, I suspect, about a number of other *Sopranos* viewers. For this critic probably isn't wrong to associate ethnicity—specifically the ethnicity of the *audience*—with the show's unusual charisma. However (and this is a big "however"), a more appropriate formulation of her claim that "You don't have to be Italian for *The Sopranos* to hit home" might be: "Most of the time you have to be *not* Italian for *The Sopranos* to hit home," just as "Most people have to be *not* Italian to feel like one of *la famiglia* watching *The Godfather.*" These works are at the very least likely to elicit ambivalence from a whole slew of the Italians—that is, the Italian *Americans*—who count themselves among the "20 million hard-working Americans" *not* associated with the Mafia. (As for Italian Italians, they play, after all, only a small part in what we might call the sociology of Media Mobsters.) But judging from the chorus of white-bread WASP acclaim with which "families" like the Sopranos and the Corleones have been met, onscreen portrayals of literal or figurative mobster kinship groups strike special chords in the hearts of the heart of our country.

What is it, though, that all those *not* Italian Americans "get" from *The Sopranos* when the show really "hits home"? And what about the Italian Americans who manage to enjoy the series even if they aren't Media Mafia wannabes—how and why do *they* get hooked?

Maybe there's a clue in the title: *The Sopranos.* Isn't it curiously confusing? Type "The Sopranos" into, say, google.com and you'll encounter a strange mishmash of web sites, ranging from full-blown fanzines for the TV series to opera pages featuring female singers with high voices. And google's responses to your query would reflect a bewilderment that I probably wasn't alone in feeling when I first heard that there was a show with this peculiar name. An *opera* soap opera? A series of diva bio-pics devoted to stars of the Met? My only personal associations with the word "soprano" were musical. In fact, in all my years of growing up Italian American I never encountered its use as a proper (last) name.

Given Chase/De Cesare's po-mo savvy, he may well have intended a pun here, though at the moment I certainly have no inclination to get entangled in the dire "intentional fallacy" that is said to plague some literary critics. For no matter what the auteur meant, he ended up with a series whose title is distinctly ambiguous, signifying (on one level) a family name, while evoking (on another level) a set of performers traditionally featured in those heightened and highly theatrical musical works we call operas.

Suppose, then, we "read" *The Sopranos* precisely as an *opera* soap opera, a kind of over-the-top psychodrama in which, as in some extravagant costume piece by Verdi or Puccini, larger-than-life characters act out plots of extraordinary vividness and violence to the accompaniment of emphatic background noises.

Because most people think of opera as Italian (*pace* [peace] Wagner and Mozart), these characters are Italians. But more to the point, these characters are Italians because many people think of Italians as *operatic*—which is to say intense, emotive, melodramatic, even histrionic. Indeed, like figures in the operas that are assumed to represent their kinds of lives, Italians seem to white-bread Americans to have precisely the "big emotions" and "messy relationships" that Millman found so enthralling in *The Sopranos.*

What happens to my three explanations of the show's popularity (with non–Italian Americans) if I push this analysis further? Since I launched into my meditation on *The Sopranos* as operatic psychodrama by conceding

Chase's po-mo savvy, I'll revisit these ideas in reverse order, starting with *The Sopranos R Postmodern Art.*

Of course whether or not *The Sopranos R Operatic,* "they" are self-consciously "postmodern," in part because of the ambiguity built into the show's title, in part because of the kind of self-reflexiveness I noted in "The Legend of Tennessee Moltisanti," in part because as the very title of that episode suggests (and as Lavery observes) the series is indeed "intertextual." But as a kind of crazy, quasi-opera, *The Sopranos R* also exceptionally postmodern because what a number of reviewers have described as the show's "complex, layered episodes" appeal to the TV equivalent of the stereotypical opera audience filled with connoisseurs who know the difference between, say, a Domingo high C, a Carreras high C, and a Pavarotti high C, and can then compare the intonations of these Three Tenors to the storied performances of Bjoerling, del Monaco, and Tagliavini—an audience, in other words, that comes with a "full breadth of cultural references."

And if *The Sopranos R Postmodern Art,* then it goes without saying that *The Sopranos R* (at least in a postmodern context) *Art.* But Caryn James isn't wrong, either, in averring that the show is "art" in yet another context. For even if the saga of the New Jersey Soprano family isn't exactly a twenty-first-century equivalent of "Zola's Rougon-Macquart series or Balzac's 'Comedie Humaine,'" it's as artful as, for instance, a series of grim Grimm fairytales set to music, which is what many operas are anyway. As a hyperbolic theatrical fantasy of familial blood-'n-guts, that is, *The Sopranos* is artful in the skill with which it simultaneously fulfills guilty as well as innocent wishes and dramatizes the fears that often collect around such wishes.

Fulfills wishes: sometimes *The Sopranos* magically offers solace to characters (and viewers) suffering from the most ordinary anxieties and irritations. Just a few examples, chosen almost at random, would include Carmela's intervention in her daughter Meadow's college application process and Christopher Moltisanti's braggadocio in a bakery where he's had to wait too long in line. In the first case, a sweetly smiling Carmela extracts a letter of reference for Meadow's Georgetown dossier from her neighbor Jean Cusamano's recalcitrant sister, a Georgetown alum, with just the slightest glint of Mafiosa steeliness ("Full Leather Jacket"). In the second, Christopher terrorizes a sales clerk who is slow in serving him by just plain shooting up the store ("The Legend of Tennessee Moltisanti"). Quotidian—maybe *un peu* Balzacian—situations, yes, but resolved through the deus ex machina, the Black Hand, as it were, of the operatic, Italian American Mob.

And resolved quite a bit more melodramatically through an even franker intercession of fairytale violence is the fate of Tony's nuisance of a brother-in-law-to-be, Richie Aprile, whose "fiancée," gangland hipster-sister Janice Soprano, up and shoots him dead when he has the nerve to slap her during a domestic squabble. (Resolved with equally fantastic mobster efficiency is the problem of Richie's corpse, which so far as I can tell is put through a meat—or garbage?—grinder by Tony's minions, and that's that.)

Okay, so who hasn't had dark fantasies about college applications, long lines in bakeries, obnoxious in-laws? That is, I suppose, one reason why besides being artful and postmodern, *The Sopranos R Us,* at least from the perspective of televiewers who don't happen to share the Italian American ethnic identity of this mythic mobster family. (Those of us who *do* share that identity know that the problems posed by hard-to-get-into colleges, crowded bakeries, and nasty in-laws aren't so easily and theatrically solved.)

But for the non–Italian American viewer I'd venture that *The Sopranos R Us* for even profounder reasons. The "big emotions" and "messy relationships"—the exaggerated, histrionic intensity—that decades of caricature have attributed to the stereotypical citizen of Italian descent make it possible for the Sopranos to enact, in a high key and as if onstage, desires and dreads associated not just with daily life in the "outside" world but with life in the heart of the family itself.

In the largest sense, the two "families" of the Mafioso boss obviously reinforce this connection with the dangerous passions inherent in the very concept of family. In smaller ways, too, the show continually unfolds a web of all-in-the-family kinship connections (e.g., Jeanne Cusamano's twin *sister* is that Georgetown alum; Tony's *sister's* boyfriend's *brother* used to be the "Capo"; Carmela tries to get it on with the *brother* of one of Tony's victims, etc.). And of course a number of characters bear names that emphasize family position—Anthony (Soprano), Jr., Jackie (Aprile), Jr., and my all-time personal favorite, Uncle *Junior* (where the "Junior," originally attached to "Corrado, Jr.," simply preempted the given name, leaving poor Uncle Junior, the house-arrested figurehead boss of both Soprano families, identified *only* by family position).

It's not just the web of family connections, though, that *The Sopranos* brings to the surface, proving that from a WASP perspective these Italian American gangster "types" *R* (the Freudian) *Us* at our most heated and hyperbolic. Primal fantasies of Father Power? How about imagining Dad as a killer—like, when you go on that innocent tour of New England colleges and he suddenly disappears for a while. Was he *murdering* somebody? Isn't that what we secretly fear he might have been doing? Or how about imagining Grandma as a poisonous witch—like, when she seems to be safely ensconced in an Assisted Living Community but really she's pulling invisible strings to off that son of hers who's so murderous in his own right? And Mom—well, let's go easy on Mom, it's too scary to think about *her*: What might she be doing with the Priest, or with the Wallpaper Man? And the mythic Uncle (who stands in for a Grandpa): Who knows what *he* does in bed? And indeed what about *Dad's* Sex Life? Who might he be banging, and where and how? Got any fantasies about that? *Bada Bing!* Yes you do, and the Sopranos will scream them out for you, all in high *C*s.

And hey, all this brilliantly staged operatic soap-opera psychodrama is so compelling that even a shrink would love it, so *The Sopranos* has a dandy one handy, counter-transference and all, to analyze the lead performer, advise him, chide him, and eventually get all hung up on his story, just the way "we" do.

Perhaps, along with the genealogical gag proffered by Uncle Junior's dazzling name, *The Sopranos'* finest *jeu* is the elaborate, extended psychiatrist joke incarnated by Dr. Jennifer Melfi, whose surgically accurate enactment by Lorraine Bracco has been rightly praised. Indeed, if I introspect with sufficient seriousness, I'd have to admit that it's ultimately been the figure of Dr. Melfi who has reconciled me to watching long swatches of this show. For even if I'd never want anyone in *my* family to speculate that *The Sopranos R Us*, I can get used to imagining that the *non*-Mafioso Italian American Dr. Melfi *is* (one of) Us, or, to be even more candid, *Dr. Melfi Is (or anyway Might Be) Me*—me watching with concern, distaste, and eventually, alas, despite some of my deepest misgivings, a kind of fascination as those "bad uncles of the barren/cliffs of Sicily" keep on stealing the show.

I write this, I have to confess, without having seen a single frame of the third season of *The Sopranos,* but I already know that though *Dr. Melfi Might Be Me,* I wouldn't want to be *her.* Counter-transference to a Mafioso, public drunkenness, rape? If I had to keep watching highlights from the Life of Dr. Melfi, I suspect that, as if I were back in the old family room watching one of the *Godfather* movies, I'd knock over the bowl of popcorn and run screaming back to my non-Mafioso kitchen.

WHY I LIKE THE WOMEN IN *THE SOPRANOS* EVEN THOUGH I'M NOT SUPPOSED TO

Regina Barreca

Carmela: *"You let him hold a gun to your head during sex? I thought you were a feminist."*
Janice: *"Yeah. . . . Well, usually he takes the clip out."*

PROLOGUE

I was the first woman in my family to go to college. I think I was actually one of the few women in my family to graduate from high school in a timely fashion. Don't get me wrong: they were very smart cookies. They were wisecracking babes with big brown eyes, wearing "Evening in Paris" perfume and a lipstick color called "Hungry Red." But they left school when they got their working papers, as was considered appropriate, and got jobs close enough to home so that they could stop by for lunch. Which they did.

Employed as telephone operators, as receptionists, as hairdressers, they worked from the day they left school until the day they got married. Not too much time passed between those dates. After that, they met one another for coffee and Ebinger's crumbcake, talked over produce at the market, and met at the playground where they watched over beautiful dark-eyed babies. A good life. They made lunch for others.

College? Nobody had ever thought about it, especially not for the girls. You can understand why my ambitions to stay in school after I got my diploma were more furtive than sex. (At least with sex, you knew you were doing what everybody else did. College was dangerous because it was unknown.) In my senior year I applied— more or less in secret—to a couple of colleges and won a scholarship. It was better than being Miss Subways. It was like being adopted by a rich relative—a concept equally unlikely.

The aunts were not impressed.

"I'm going to COLLEGE, Aunt Josie!" I yelped as I galloped downstairs to the kitchen in the cellar when the official acceptance letter arrived.

A short white-haired woman, wide as she was tall, perpetually adorned by her floral print housedress, a woman whose figure resembled nothing so much as an ottoman (the only thing missing was a button on the top of her head), eyed me briefly. After a long pause and with deep suspicion, she replied.

"You what?"

"I'm going to COLLEGE!! On a SCHOLARSHIP! I can't BELIEVE IT!"

She didn't believe it either. That much was becoming clear. She continued to speak slowly, as if talking to a foreigner.

"And just where you going to college, Gina?"

"I'm going to a place called Dartmouth in New Hampshire!" I nodded vigorously to jump-start what I imagined was her merely latent enthusiasm.

"You gonna go to New Hampshire?" she repeated, stressing every word.

"Yeah! Isn't it great?" I couldn't understand why she met my excitement with silence. Usually she was the most immediately supportive of all three tiny aunts who colonized the three-story house where my grandmother lived. Aunt Josie wasn't exactly looking at me with the benevolence of the fat fairy-godmothers in Disney's Cinderella, characters who had always secretly reminded me of female relatives.

"Here, look!" I bounced over to her. "Look at the letter!"

Josie, sighing, ignored the envelope but spent a long time looking me up and down. She also kept stirring the gravy. (The same pot had been on the stove since 1952. The gravy got better every day. We had it for lunch if we were lucky.)

Shaking her head sadly after a minute or so, Josie finally pronounced, "You're pregnant, right?"

It shouldn't have surprised me. After all, the only reason any girl had ever left the neighborhood was because she was knocked up. The girls were said to be "visiting relatives in Pennsylvania." Nobody had relatives in Pennsylvania. Nobody had relatives who lived more than twelve blocks away.

"No, no, Aunt Josie, this is good. It'll be a great opportunity for me. It'll be wonderful!" I waved the letter and envelope under her nose, for proof.

"It's okay, Gina," Aunt Josie said softly, once again ignoring the paperwork (who trusted paperwork?) as she turned back to the pot. She shrugged her shoulders in resignation. "It's not the end of the world," she whispered, finally. "It happened to your cousin Luci. Don't say I told you. Anyway, it doesn't matter. You can always come back when it's all over."

I needed all the courage I could get as I walked across the Dartmouth campus. It was September of 1975 and not only was I part of one of the first classes admitting women; as far as I could tell, the only person whose name ended in a vowel to graduate from this institution had been named "Michael Corleone." And he was fictional.

But I wasn't too worried. I knew that I had nine months before anybody expected me home.

And I knew if I came home in time for lunch, there would be gravy.

I identify with the women created by David Chase and his writers for two central reasons: because they are familiar and because they are unpredictable. These two elements are rarely paired in the development of women on television or in film. If the female characters run to types we know—the elderly mother, the cuckolded wife, the recently educated daughter—we imagine we can predict precisely how they will react within any framework (the mother will weep and cringe in fear of abandonment, the wife will condone and submit because she cannot look after herself, the daughter will arrive at a new understanding of her parents' merit and worth).

When we meet these characters in *The Sopranos,* however, all bets are off: the elderly mother arranges to have her son whacked for putting her in a retirement community; upon discovering her husband waist-deep in infidelity, the wife embarks on a shopping spree while at a four-star hotel in Rome (leaving her mobster husband in charge of car-pooling the kids and arranging for their tennis lessons); the pampered daughter goes to Columbia University, quickly loses her virginity to her half-Jewish, half–African American R. A., and learns to despise her father not only for his lack of ethics but for his lack of sophistication.

You don't find this full menu of behaviors in many other television shows. When I watch *The Sopranos,* it's as if I'm watching a documentary about my relatives—except, of course, for the Mafioso business and money stuff.

Which, as far as I am concerned, are the least interesting parts of *The Sopranos.* While learning about the inner workings of organized crime is stimulating in an anthropological sort of way, like learning about the intricacies of bee-keeping, it's not what keeps viewers tuning in every week. Yes, some objects are stolen. Some poker is played. Certain people are killed. But all that comes under the heading of "collateral damage."

It is the harrowing psychological recklessness, the relentless rush of emotional fireworks, the uncompromising believability and juicy precariousness of the characters' inner lives that make the show impossible not to watch—and, once watched, impossible not to respect.

I have found myself identifying with almost every female character in *The Sopranos* at some point during the first three seasons. Occasionally this happens against my will; often it happens against my better judgment. But it does happen—and I'm not the only woman I know who feels this way.

When Carmela yells at her son for smoking weed in the garage during his gala confirmation party, a world of maternal frustration is mobilized when she shouts "Act like a good Catholic for fifteen fucking minutes. Is that so much to ask?" When Tony Soprano challenges his psychiatrist, Dr. Jennifer Melfi, with the question "Is this a woman thing? You ask me what I'm thinking and I tell you and then you torture me with it?" you don't have to be Italian to get the full force and sweeping impact of gender-difference be-

hind the line. When Meadow won't let her father get away with a disingenu-
ous comparison of his life to his neighbor's ("You never seen Doc Cusamano
going out at three in the morning on a call?"), but instead calls him on the
incongruity of their actual positions ("Did the Cusamano kids ever find
$50,000 in krugerrands and a .45 automatic while they were hunting for
Easter eggs?"), you see illustrated the intelligence, wit, and the absolute refusal to be played for a sucker that is emblematic of *The Sopranos'* female
characters.

When he needs to organize his complicated and potentially deadly outer
life, Tony Soprano deals in a straightforward manner with his male colleagues and companions. He does not seem to have much patience for the
self-help movement (telling somebody at a party to read *Tomato Sauce for the
Ass:* "It's the Italian version of *Chicken Soup for the Soul*"). Maestro over this
male chorus, Tony occupies familiar and controllable ground. As have many
dominant male figures before him, Tony scrapes his emotional and spiritual
life off the bottom of his shoes before entering the world of men. If he feels
weak, he cannot show it without jeopardizing his authority and his life; if he
shows any ambivalence toward an action or while making a decision, he risks
forfeiting the right to rule.

Not to say that the male characters we meet are totally one dimensional,
but it is true that most of the men in *The Sopranos* appear to overcome easily
whatever second thoughts they might have about what they do. Even Tony
falls back on the catechism of "Soldiers don't go to hell. It's business, we're
soldiers, we follow codes, orders" when asked by Dr. Melfi what he thinks of
his chances in the afterlife. It's as if sins committed in his line of work do not
get added up on the soul's scoreboard. (This is also presumably what Tony
tells himself after Carmela, ostensibly attempting to reassure him during an
MRI, blurts out in frustration, "What's different between you and me is that
you're going to hell when you die.")

Interestingly enough, the men in Tony's organization are surprisingly accepting of the fact that Tony has decided to see a shrink after suffering from
panic attacks. Paulie Walnuts, the most brutal of the soldiers in Tony's
regime, is more than understanding; he also offers witness to his own experience: "It's not the worst thing I ever heard. I was seeing a therapist myself
about a year ago. I had some issues. Enough said. I learned some coping
skills." And Bada Bing owner Silvio Dante agrees that getting professional

help is probably the right move: "Look, this thing of ours, the way it's going, it'd be better if we could admit to each other these painful, stressful times. But it'll never fucking happen."

When you start to ask painful, stressful questions—when, in other words, you begin to live an examined life—you must venture into the realm of the feminine. When contemplation eats into his spirit like rust, Tony turns to women for help. And we, the viewers, are not surprised. Women own the life of the mind and the world of the emotions in *The Sopranos*. That's their turf, their "thing." It is women who have embedded the deep and enduring values of this culture. They carry within them and carry on the rituals of a personal and family life. Tony's most hazardous negotiation with a truly threatening world—where he has to confront the primordial, the unexplored, the barbaric, and the cataclysmic—is when he must go through women to get what he needs.

Non–Italian American women are as mesmerized by the complex mix of love and rage, intelligence and self-destructiveness, hunger and insatiability in the likes of Carmela, Dr. Jennifer Melfi, and Janice as those raised in the tribe. But Italian American women are in particular need of representation because there have been so few distinctly individual, high-voltage versions of Italian American women presented in either film or on television that you would think no one had ever imagined such a creature might exist. There is a dearth, especially, of intelligent and impressive—let alone educated—Italian American women represented by and in the media.

Perhaps most telling, Carmela and Dr. Melfi do not pretend to foolishness, helplessness, or innocence, those twinned weapons of the traditional passive-aggressive feminine script perfected by Livia Soprano, Tony's mother. Unlike more ordinary heroines, most of the women in *The Sopranos* do not offer up a gooey reservoir of sympathy, vulnerability, and virginity but instead offer in their place a sense of intelligent awareness, emotional skill, and a sense of shamelessness about their own competence. They do not, in other words, apologize for being good at what they do.

When I was growing up, I could choose to model myself after Annette Funicello (whom I frankly adored because of her great smile, great figure, and ability to keep the cute boys in line); the mother from "Marty" (whose most memorable line is: "These college girls. They're only one step from the street"); or Connie Francis (who, while playing a college student in *Where the Boys Are* was not the sharpest knife in the drawer, ending up with Frank Gorshen instead of George Hamilton and what kind of inspiration is that?). Later on we had the choice of projecting ourselves onto Cher or Olympia Dukakis from *Moonstruck,* neither of whom plays a character you could call truly multidimensional (and neither of whom is, in her own life, Italian American). Marisa Tomei did a great job in *My Cousin Vinny,* but she didn't exactly break new ground in terms of a depiction of a fast-talking, street-savvy Brooklyn babe (not that there's anything wrong with that).

And what did important male Italian American writers and directors give women in terms of mirrors? Scorsese gave us his fabulously familiar mother, fabulously powerful non–Italian American women, and a string of scary, inarticulate, half-crazy women who are either Italian American or attached to an Italian American man. In faithfully adapting Mario Puzo's *The Godfather,* Coppola gave us out-of-control, needs-her-brother Connie Corleone, a beautiful, early-dying, and unspeaking first wife for Michael, and ultimately his WASPy convert-to-Catholicism second wife, Kay.

Is it surprising, then, that I'm attracted to the trio of Dr. Melfi, Carmela Soprano, and Meadow Soprano—three college-educated women? That even Tony's sister, cunning, insecure, ex-hippy Janice; ambitious, naive, and under-educated Adriana; and independent, high-minded, and desperate Charmaine hold appeal?

You don't get to see powerful, interesting, multifaceted, serious depictions of Italian American women on any screen of any size. Thirty years ago you had the competitive, smothering mom in "Marty" and now you've got the competitive, smothering mom in "Everybody Loves Raymond." These mother-figures are pretty much alike and, despite an edginess to both created by the excellent actresses playing their roles, their characters are unapologetically one-dimensional and benignly comical.

Livia Soprano, in contrast, isn't benign; she is fiendishly malignant. "Everybody thought Dad was the ruthless one but I gotta hand it to you, Ma," admits Tony, "If you'd been born after these feminists, you would've been the real gangster." With the curious power of the totally self-absorbed, Livia is what Freudian critics might call the classic "phallic-mother," the maternal figure who rules over and wields all the weapons provided by the patriarchal realm. Livia took her children's love and held it over them like a whip.

Her children adored Livia but couldn't let her know it, because they knew she would think them weak and try to use their love to manipulate or damage them even further. Simone de Beauvoir, in her classic work *The Second Sex,* anticipates the characterization of deadly feminine weakness crystallized in Livia Soprano: "[She] lies in wait like the carnivorous plant," passive and lethal. "She is absorption, suction, humus, pitch and glue, a passive influx, insinuating and viscous." The patriarchal matriarch is scary: she batters those around her into action while seeming only to beguile them with the powers of the weak and thereby effectively disguises her iron maiden malevolence.[1]

Carmela recognizes Livia's camouflaged strength for what it is and tells her mother-in-law, "This 'poor mother, nobody loves me' victim crap . . . is textbook manipulation. And I hate seeing Tony so upset over it. I know how to talk to people. I am a mother too, don't forget. You know the power that you have. And you use it like a pro." Livia can only stutter, "Power? What power? I don't have power. I'm a shut-in," but Carmela won't let her pass off this cheap reproduction of helplessness as the real thing. "You're bigger than life. You are his mother," insists Carmela, "I don't think for one second that you don't know what you're doing to him."

When Livia is funny, she doesn't mean to be. To laugh at her is to reduce her power. When she inadvertently runs over her best friend in her driveway, for example, we are not laughing with Livia, we are definitely laughing at her, even with authentic horror. Laughing at an old woman no longer in control of her actions? It is a comic scene nevertheless because this is one act of violence Livia did not mean to commit. Her character is so unappetizing that you find yourself longing for the exposure of her true self at any cost. Besides, running down her friends is not Livia's style (we later see that claimed by Richie Aprile); emotional and psychological violence are Livia's forte.

As Carmela says, Livia is a pro. One scene with her grandson offers a brilliant illustration: Having picked up some ideas about existentialism from school the way a dark suit picks up lint, Anthony Junior asks grandmother whether the world holds any meaning. Rather than offer platitudes or comfort, Livia barks, "It's all a big nothing. What makes you think you're so special?" The startling incongruity between the set-up (a bed-ridden granny visited in the hospital by her youngest grandchild is asked for her thoughts on the meaning of life) and the payoff ("The world is a jungle—if you want

my advice, don't expect happiness . . . in the end you die in your own arms")
is a magnificently crafted piece of mockery.

We laugh in scorn at Livia as we might laugh at the evil witch being
pushed into the oven at the end of "Hansel and Gretel." *The Sopranos,* more
often than not, appears to be divided between encouraging its audience in
the impulse to laugh aloud and the equally seductive impulse to burst into
scornful invective. Perhaps one of the distinctive features of *The Sopranos* is
its ability to combine effectively the need for laughter and the need for invective. Livia, therefore, can be seen as an object of scorn because of the manner
in which her recreational self-pity is coupled with her remorseless vindictive-
ness. But it is clear that Livia occupies an entirely different narrative space
from her harmless television predecessors and her film counterparts.

When Livia feels competitive and smothering, she does not offer a
clownish display of antagonism about a daughter-in-law's ability to enchant
or inability to cook. The whole idea of a "smothering" maternal presence is
embodied and literalized by Livia, who screams, "I'd rather smother them
with a pillow than take them to Nevada" when asked by her husband if she'd
be willing to move out to Reno. Livia isn't kidding, either. When she threatens to kill her kids, you know she means it. No character from a Greek
tragedy is needed to make those lines ring: they echo down the low-ceilinged
hallways of two-family houses throughout the tri-state area.

When, many years later, Livia feels triumphant over the fact that her
daughter Janice will not marry Richie Aprile, she announces, "He probably
jilted her—that's the story of her life." Tony, standing up for his sister as a
psychological substitution for standing up for himself, counters with a question, as applicable to himself as to his sister, which remains impossible for
Livia to answer: "What kind of a fucking chance did she have with you as her
mother?"

Livia is the mother of nightmares, the pitiful, dependent, unloving woman
who demands but never offers pity, support, or love. Her rejection of every
feminine (compassionate, unselfish, non-manipulative) or positive (intelligent,
sophisticated, thoughtful, caring) possible action or answer is indicative of
Livia's uncontrolled and uncontrollable presence in *The Sopranos*. It is indicative of the danger Livia represents to the very systems that try to silence her. Violent, destructive, and murderous, Livia crosses a cultural and social
demarcation beyond which she will find herself excluded. The family's perime-

ter is emotionally policed by the forces of Carmela and Livia. Within its core is the figure of Tony—a man belonging to both, and to neither, of them.

Courageous enough to braid together the domestic and the sexual, the educated and the nurturing, the machiavellian and the maternal, the vindictive and the compassionate, the good and the evil, Chase clears new ground for the women. Neither madonnas nor whores (even the whores are not your ordinary whores—they too have complicated inner lives), the female characters in *The Sopranos* make life difficult for their men—and for their viewers, even those of us who identify with them.

Livia sets the pace for the other women in David Chase's television program because of her complexity: the women play roles that are difficult to categorize but impossible to overlook. Livia is entirely believable even if she is not commonplace. Chase accomplishes what other writers have rarely attempted in the creation of female characters who are neither stereotypes nor anomalies.

Not, of course, that the show is without its critics. When I hear commentators sneer that the character of Livia Soprano is an unbelievable portrait of the monstrous mother or that (as one academic colleague put it) "Livia's bitterness and malevolence cannot be regarded as anything but cartoonish," I am amazed. When critics ungenerously reduce Chase's accomplishment to a list of stock-figures and buffoons, I am always astonished. I knew Livia; she was one of those aunts I described earlier. (She was the aunt who, when I asked her for the definition of "vendetta"—a word I didn't understand during her conversation with one of my other relatives—she paused briefly, then explained matter-of-factly, "'Vendetta' is Italian for 'Are you seeing other women?'") And when Tony Soprano hisses "she has a fucking smile on her face" when Livia is being wheeled on a stretcher to St. Vincent's, we know he is right in his observation: Livia's smile is the smile of one who has the last laugh.

Put it this way: the women in Sopranoland are types who do not run to type. While they occupy familiar narrative positions around the male characters, and while they look exactly as you think they would, they do not act, talk, feel, or believe the way we anticipate. Not one of the women in *The Sopranos* is a role model. They are not meant to be, but neither are they merely background figures arranged for decoration or convenience. This is neither an issue of *Ms.* nor of Italian *Vogue.* These are everyday women from New Jersey. From everywhere.

They are women who struggle with what it means to be both smart and independent yet desperately long for love and acceptance. They want to succeed but not be too successful. They want control over their own lives—so long as they can keep one foot in the world they know as they venture into the unknown. They crave security and yet despise the thought that their safety depends on the favors of someone else. In other words, they want what everybody wants. Dr. Melfi with her Ph.D., Carmela with her book club, Janice with her self-esteem issues—these are women we know. These are women we are. Of course we find them fascinating.

And of course *we* know, even if the guys don't, just how dangerous they are. The women in *The Sopranos* are, without a doubt, at least as deadly as the males—in some cases, literally, in other cases, metaphorically. Livia, Carmela, Dr. Melfi, and Janice are more dangerous than Junior, Tony, Christopher, and Paulie because the women commandeer power while seeming to wield none. The evidence of their powers of destruction is more easily disguised. In other words, while the women might have to stoop to conquer, they do eventually and efficiently conquer their enemies. They are victorious at almost every level. You don't want to get on their bad side.

The strength and the sustaining force, ultimately, behind these female characters lies not in their gender or sexuality per se but in the fact that they command access to the centers of social and cultural structures, even as they might be seen as undermining these structures by their very presence. Carmela has the diplomacy of a U.N. official, the deportment of a cabinet member's consort, and the social ambitions of a CEO's wife. The women are unassimilable because of where they started and who they are, and yet, paradoxically, they are wholly infiltrating the homes of the ruling class. When Carmela walks into the fancy attorney's office of Jean Cusamano's sister in order to procure a letter of recommendation to Georgetown for Meadow, she comes carrying a ricotta pie—which, for a woman like Carmela, is the equivalent of coming "heavy." She insists that Joan do her the favor she requests: "I don't think you understand. I want you to write that letter. . . . Don't make me beg here." When the lawyer's sister Jean, Carmela's neighbor, returns the dish from the pie, she gushingly tells Carmela that the letter was written. Carmela smiles warmly—and asks for a copy.

The women in *The Sopranos* embrace, and simultaneously dilute, the respected rituals of the legitimate world. If anything, the women in this world have an additional burden: they are required to have a more public role to play than many of their non–Italian American counterparts. Unlike many families, in which the husband is the representative of the outside, external world, the women in these households have more ability, mobility, and access to the "legit" world than the men who cannot face the world as who they truly are without risking incarceration or death.

Let's return to Carmela's confirmation party for her son, Anthony Junior. Priests rub shoulders with hit men; legit families sit down to dinner with the Mob and nobody gets indigestion. The humor of such scenes—and there are a number of them—underscores rather than undermines the socially disruptive nature of Chase's characters. You can't tell the legit and illegit partygoers apart. Carmela is adept at intermingling the various aspects of her life in a way that serves to erase, or at least blur, the superficially irreconcilable worlds of the "legit" and "illegit," and by so doing confuses the boundaries between the two. A similar point is made by Meadow during the conversation in which she confronts Tony about his role in organized crime. Because her father is honest with her—at least partially—she rewards him by explaining that he is no worse than many other fathers: "Sometimes I wish you were like other dads. But then, like . . . Mr. Scangarelo for example? An advertising executive for big tobacco. Or lawyers? So many dads are full of shit." Chase has created a little pocket of social, political, and cultural anarchy and gleefully intends to enjoy it.

Chase does not force his characters to rely on a subtext that, like a brass rubbing, requires further art for the central figures to be brought into relief. The women of *The Sopranos* do not rely on double-talk to assure themselves a respectable position in the social order; they are already exiled from being able to appropriate that position for themselves because of their family ties. At several points in the narrative, for example, Carmela questions whether she has the right to use Tony's "blood money" (as one therapist calls it) to make her small world better. Does being financially dependent on Tony make her, as this psychiatrist argues, an "accomplice"? Is she encouraging Meadow to replicate her behavior when she cautions her daughter, "I would hate to think you're airing your family's business in public"?

Should Carmela force Tony to cough up the $50,000 requested by the dean of Columbia University, who explains, "It's what the Giving Committee felt you would be comfortable with," and which Carmela regards as a way to keep Meadow in the best position the university can offer? When Tony responds to Carmela's request from the "legit" world (in this case, the refined fraternity of Ivy League schools) in the vernacular of his own—"Fifty grand? You gotta be kidding me . . . [they're] holding her hostage. I won't pay. I know too much about extortion"—Carmela is as adamant as she can be. She, therefore, responds in his vernacular. The more Carmela understands about her husband's life, the freer she becomes to spend money as she sees fit, and the less accountable she feels for how she allocates her own spending money. "All the money" that Tony pays out, she retorts, "[a]nd there's not enough to make sure your own daughter is protected?" Even when Tony argues that the dean is merely trying to "shake him down," Carmela persists.

That Carmela makes these demands of Tony illustrates more of an interest in the delineation of her conflicting identity than it shows any immediate eagerness to amend her ways. Carmela has, as she tells her bitter mother, "earned" her keep; if "the waters part . . . wherever [she] goes," Carmela has already paid the price for this privilege. She tests the reactions of those around her in order to gauge rather than to change the effect she has on them; she, like Livia, knows her family well. Unlike Livia, however, Carmela genuinely loves them. This does not mean, however, that she cannot be driven to extremes. And sometimes these extremes *will* make her seem more, rather than less, like the passive-aggressive and traditionally feminine women around her.

So when Carmela, wrapped in a quilt, is lying on the couch when Tony comes home, he knows there is something profoundly wrong. Carmela's M.O. is not one of retreat and surrender. When she answers his inquiry about why she's lying down in the afternoon, Carmela replies without apparent anger, "Everybody else in this family sleeps all day. I thought I would try it." Her declaration contains a barely submerged undercurrent of resentment at the fact that she, and she alone, has kept it cohesive, struggling to maintain the bonds and rituals that keep them within the orbit of her influence—an influence that keeps the family whole.

It is not surprising, then, that Carmela is ecstatic when Tony reveals that he's been to see a therapist for his panic attacks. She is so excited that her husband is taking some responsibility for his own emotional well-being that he becomes embarrassed and tells her to "Take it easy." Carmela is willing to risk alienation from him in order to have a more honest and richer emotional life with him and so she welcomes whatever soul-searching he can accomplish in the care of a therapist. At this point, of course, Carmela is not aware of the fact that Dr. Melfi is a woman.

The idea that Tony Soprano sees a shrink—and a female shrink at that—is the paradox that mystifies and holds the viewers. Even when his associates shrug off the fact that Tony is seeking psychiatric help, they have trouble dealing with the gender issue: "Paulie saw a shrink, not a woman. I couldn't get past that." It's as if the "shrink" part and the "woman" part cancel each other out, as if those roles cannot simultaneously co-exist within one person.

Interestingly enough, a similar dynamic is at work with Annalisa, the Italian woman who heads the crime family Tony and his crew meet in Naples. However astute and powerful Annalisa appears, it is clearly unsettling to Tony's crew to take a powerful woman seriously. "A fucking woman boss?" is the reaction from the American men. Annalisa explains succinctly: "Our men kill each other . . . or they go to prison. The men are in love with their mommas, so obeying a woman comes naturally." Her logic is impeccable. So is her mastery over the demands of those who refuse to grant her authority. When Tony becomes fed up with her and demands to deal with her husband, Annalisa is uncompromising: "You have to fucking deal with me." Annalisa even reminds him of Melfi; he later tells his therapist, "When I was in Italy, I met a woman who reminded me of you—one of these witchy broads—told me I was my own worst enemy."

Initially Tony hides from Carmela the fact that the therapist he's seeing is a woman. In part he dissimulates because he himself cannot find the language to represent the unresolved tensions in the therapeutic relationship. Only when Dr. Melfi calls Tony at home to cancel an appointment does Carmela discover the secret of Melfi's sex. She is less than thrilled and displays as much in what for Carmela is a rare show of anger, jealousy, and vulgarity.

"She didn't know you were a girl," Tony explains rather sheepishly to Dr. Melfi, trying to help her understand Carmela's furious response to the phone call. He catches himself on the word "girl" and, stuttering, attempts a corrective by offering, "didn't know you were a woman." He pauses. "A doctor." Another brief pause. "A woman doctor." Although Tony has a tricky time figuring out how to award a suitably descriptive, precise, and unpatronizing name to what Jennifer Melfi is, we of course are not at all surprised that Tony has chosen a woman as his therapist. Melfi poses the question directly: "Why a woman?" she asks Tony. He answers honestly, no hesitations and pauses. He was offered a choice by his doctor and next-door neighbor Cusamano, between "two Jewish guys and a paesan like me." Turning the question back toward Dr. Melfi, Tony asks why she didn't avoid him. "You, you didn't flinch," he points out with a conspiratorial grin. She smiles. "Most 'legit' people would have run the other way."

Not that there is an absence of conflict in their relationship. Like Annalisa, Melfi needs to have her authority firmly established from the outset. Gently but firmly she corrects him when he asks, "What part of the boot are you from, hon?" "Dr. Melfi," she insists, and from that point onward he never calls her "hon" again. When Tony begins to bring them both cups of coffee, she points out that, as kindly as the gesture is meant, it would be inappropriate for her to accept gifts. Her tone is polite but unyielding. She is an enigma to Tony, a page so blank he can fill her with his own thoughts. Jennifer Melfi does not appear that way to us, the viewers: we see her own troubled home life, we have access to a fuller sense of her humanity than she permits her patient.

Tony becomes increasingly attracted to his therapist. This is perhaps most poignantly manifested in a scene with his Russian mistress, Irina. After casually suggesting to Irina that she wear more "professional"-looking clothing in what is clearly an attempt to make her over in Melfi's image, he then makes a more drastic and telling blunder. Instead of just getting down to the sexual act, Tony wants to make conversation. We see, in a way that Tony does not, the predicament at the heart of his dilemma: He wants to talk to his mistress and have sex with his therapist. There's a whole lot of transference going on.

When he finally admits that he loves her, Tony still does not address Dr. Melfi directly by name. "I love you . . . I'm in love with you . . . it's just the way it is." Remaining detached, kind, and professional, she explains the familiar dynamics of the situation: "I've been a broad, generic, sympathetic woman to you because that's what this work calls for." Tony's declaration of affection comes, fittingly enough, soon after a moment of genuine intimacy—a burst of laughter—breaks through the professional persona within which Dr. Melfi envelops herself. Seemingly comfortable inside her professional mask, which she wears as lightly and as elegantly as her tailored suits, she gently questions Tony about the possible physiological causes of his recent bout of impotence, asking "Have you ever had a prostate exam?" When Tony immediately wisecracks "Are you kidding? I don't let anyone wag their finger in my FACE," she loses control and laughs outright. The look on his face is one of unmitigated delight. He is delighted as she covers her mouth in embarrassment, and while trying unsuccessfully to reclaim her sense of decorum, she says "I shouldn't laugh." Fumbling blindly into new emotions, Tony—not long after this scene—asks Irina to wear a suit and talk to him about his day.

Dr. Melfi, although intimidated by Tony and aware of his violent nature, nevertheless continues to make Tony work hard for his therapeutic payola. She tosses tough question after tough question at him and refuses, except for that early lapse, to permit his humor to deflect the seriousness of their work together. "What's the one thing every woman—your mother, your wife, your daughter—have in common?" Dr. Melfi asks. When Tony instantly replies, "They all break my balls," she does not laugh, but instead helps him move to the next realization. "They're all Italian," she points out, encouraging him to see that, in choosing her for his therapist, he chooses once more to let an Italian American woman into his life.

Dr. Melfi also stresses the ways in which Tony's predicaments are not sui generis: "Grown children often secretly wish for an aged parent to die," declares Dr. Melfi and, in one of her most remarkable lines, adds, "And it's not necessary for the parent to be a witness for the prosecution." But neither does she allow him to forget or skip over the parts of his life that are indeed unconventional. In another session, as Tony is describing a sexual dream about his neighbor Jean Cusamano ("I finish, you know. And her big ass is . . ."), he breaks off and insists, "Look, we don't have time for this shit." But Dr. Melfi, who knows the Cusamanos socially, has her attention caught by a physical detail. "It's interesting that you would say a big ass, because Jean is quite slender." In response to her question, Tony both gruffly and wryly insists, "We've got bigger things to talk about than Jean Cusamano's ass." In this instance, Dr. Melfi does not fall for the punchline. Instead she counters with a blow straight to the heart: "Like feelings of worthlessness sparked by your mother's plot to have you killed?"

One of the most unnervingly brutal scenes in a television series shaded, nuanced, and sometimes filled with brutality involved Dr. Melfi. And it did not—at least not up to the moment of this writing—involve any figure from organized crime. When news commentators and editorial writers began to complain in earnest over the increasing violence in *The Sopranos,* their remarks came not after the episode in which one of Tony's main men was killed by his friends, not after the murder of a stupid boy who wanted to impress the mobsters but fouled up, but instead after the rape of Jennifer Melfi in a stairwell outside her office. Ugly, repulsive, painful, and reprehensible, the violence of the rape was garishly underscored by revulsion and disgust, not arousal or desire.

Why did the unsentimental depiction of a rape under the klieg lights of the random hatred that clearly motivated it profoundly shock a viewing audience left repeatedly unshocked by murder? Because of some lingering fondness for a myth that positions the rapist as merely a passionate seducer? Because Dr. Melfi screamed and cried out in the throat-tearing howl of an animal being attacked? Because we wanted Tony to ride in, just before things went too far, to rescue her? Because Tony should have, at this crucial moment, turned into the "knight in white satin armor" Irina (as well as his wife, his daughter, and his sisters) always wanted him to be?

To begin with, it seems clear that the nature of this one scene distinguished it from other acts of physical violence depicted in the show because it was played out against a "civilian," someone who has no direct connection to organized crime. Melfi is one of "us," in other words, someone who knows Tony and Carmela Soprano only through one carefully limited and boundaried relationship, not someone who benefits from their patronage or depends on their good wishes. Justifying the savagery in the world of the Mob (as the program implicitly does when, for example, it turns out that the ex-mobster Tony kills in Maine was still dealing hard drugs) is standard issue, part of the catechism Tony chanted earlier—"It's business, we're soldiers."

But the rape of Dr. Melfi is committed by a local kid named Jesus Rossi, a surname that, as Dr. Melfi's on-again, off-again husband Richard points out, "sounds Italian." Rossi is not only caught by the police, he is released by the police because some procedural paperwork had gone awry during the early stages of the criminal investigation. Sputtering banalities and disastrously ineffective, both Melfi's husband and son are inept and powerless.

When she sees her own therapist, Melfi permits the contempt she feels toward all these legit men in her life to show: "Who's gonna stop him, you?" Melfi's vitriolic confession—when she describes to her psychiatrist a dream in which a Rottweiler, clearly a substitution for Tony, attacks her attacker— hints that her respect for the legit world might be in danger of collapse. She hisses at her doctor, "Let me tell you something: no feeling has ever been so sweet as to see that pig beg and plead and scream for his life because the justice system is fucked up." If she lets Tony off the leash in terms of avenging her, she can guarantee herself a ringside seat at the undoing of her rapist. But does she want this? Do *we* want this?

Do we want, in other words, for Dr. Melfi to become as emotionally unprincipled, as emotionally invested, as wrought-up as Tony's sister Janice? Janice, too, was subjected to violence—her abuser was the man she lived with and whom she had permitted to hold a gun to her head during sex. Janice was punched by Richie Aprile, the man she would have married—that is, if she had not shot him after he belted her hard across the mouth and then sat down again to resume his dinner. This was another scene provoking a gender-specific response: the next day's conversation around the water-cooler heard many men saying that Janice was nuts and had drastically overreacted and equally as many women saying they hadn't watched such a satisfying response to domestic violence since *Thelma and Louise.*

Janice resembles Livia in that she is neurotic, caustic, manipulative, and irresponsible, bent on attributing to others the failures and problems of her own life and blind to her own part in the creation of these problems. She resembles her brother Tony insofar as she appreciates the strength and force of money, the relative power of weapons, the importance of allies and allegiances. Like Tony, Janice has learned the hard way. She has learned that the pretty ways taught to privileged little girls will not work for her. Learning partly from experience and partly from instinct, Janice comes to the conclusion that it is in her interest to challenge, rather than observe or submit to, the world around her. In response, she goes to extremes: Janice steals the prosthetic device from a one-legged woman, for example, and remains unapologetic—until she is coerced (by some carefully applied force) to divulge the hiding place of the fake leg.

But unlike the men in her world, Janice is capable of checking and delaying her automatic responses. Janice can anticipate as well as store grievances. She can also revert to the family's talent for echoing the passive voice, the voice refusing to assign personal responsibility: a year or so after Janice shoots her ex-fiance, she whines, "I was supposed to be married at this point in my life." It's as if she is an ingenue sighing over a long-lost love. "Yeah, so?" asks Tony, eyebrows raised ("This should be a good one" is written all over his face). Janice, without any trace of irony and with all the pathos she can possibly muster, laments, "The man I love died."

Yet I believe that Janice, even with her terrible judgment, would have known better than to trust Gloria. Ah, Gloria: the reincarnation and embodiment of the worst of Livia. Gloria: Mercedes saleslady, an Italian American woman who has sex in the python house at the zoo, a woman Tony meets in Dr. Melfi's waiting room, who, Tony tells his therapist, is "smart, sexy . . . Italian . . . she's actually nothing like you. Well, maybe a little." Gloria, he insists, makes him a "better husband and a better father." Being with Gloria makes him happier "than all your therapy and all your Prozac combined," he taunts. Dr. Melfi pushes Tony to attempt other layers of recognition. "Who else" does Gloria remind him of? asks Dr. Melfi; what other woman in Tony's life, she asks, had a "depressive personality," was "unstable, impossible to please?" "What attracted you to Gloria in the first place?" Dr. Melfi asks. Or Irina before her? "Does [she] remind you of any other woman?" Despite the fact that Tony becomes dizzy in Gloria's presence (an indication of the onset of one of his panic attacks), he denies being able to forge any connection. Not that he isn't worried. He asks Dr. Melfi if Gloria is "a full blown loop-de-loop?"

It is only when Gloria actually echoes the voluptuously destructive self-pity of Livia's rants that Tony understands who he's found. Only after she cries, "I'll sit back like a mute while you screw every woman out there" and "nobody cares if I'm alive or dead" and "kill me" does Tony hear the resonance—Livia also said everyone would be happier if she were "a mute," as well as moaning that she (and everyone else) would be "better off dead." When Gloria becomes hysterical, calling Tony at home and threatening to tell Carmela about their affair (note: she had already met Carmela, having secretly arranged to take Carmela for a [literal] ride in a demonstration model Mercedes), Tony hears through the hysteria the voice that has always been there: the voice of his mother. "I didn't just meet you," Tony recoils in recognition, "I've known you my whole fucking life. . . . My mother was just like you . . . [a] bottomless black hole."

Confronting Gloria, who at this point is arrayed in the full bloom of her pathology—having begged Tony to kill her, having thrown all the dishes on the floor, having flung an entire London Broil at Tony's head—Tony spits at his mistress the words he never quite said to his mother: "You're fucking crazy . . . you're a dangerous fuck and I don't want you in my life." Therapy has evidently paid off for Tony Soprano. It brought him to the edge of the abyss by introducing him to Gloria—and gave him the ability and strength to refuse to be suckered by her deadly psychological scam.

"She wanted me to kill her . . . she saw me as a fucking hammer?" Tony asks Dr. Melfi in genuine horror. Dr. Melfi, in turn, asks Tony, "How did you recognize in Gloria this deeply wounded angry being underneath who would let you . . . try to win the love of your mother?" With Gloria's "incessant self-regard," Tony could have easily been conned into believing that this is what real love was like, because "in your mother's hands, it passed for love."

"You'll never leave your wife . . . you made one good decision in your life vis-à-vis women. You're not going to throw that over," Dr. Melfi reassures Tony, in part because "in spite of everything, you're a very conventional man."

Surrounded by unconventional women. If Tony, through the process of examining his life, is to discover that there is no happiness, no contentment, no fully lived life to be found in the outward order of things, in the external world of money, men, and violence, then perhaps he will also learn that only those who can draw from some inner source can survive. If he learns this, he will learn it from the women in his life: from the women sitting in the analysts' chairs, from the ones talking to him and helping him through, from the ones who struggle with the idea of unconditional love, from the ones stirring the pots of gravy.

WONDERBREAD AND STUGOTS

ITALIAN AMERICAN MANHOOD
AND *THE SOPRANOS*

E. Anthony Rotundo

The tiles of the Holland Tunnel flicker past. The car emerges into day-light on the Jersey side and the New York skyline appears through the passenger window. The New Jersey Turnpike looms ahead—the city skyline shifts to the rearview mirror and recedes. The industrial landmarks of the Jersey Meadowlands flash by and the scale becomes more human—a church, a cemetery, a muffler shop, Satriales's, a pizza place, a series of neighbor-hoods, a gate in a wall, a long driveway, a big house.

The journey that Tony Soprano takes at the start of every episode of *The Sopranos* is not a commuter trip. It is a ritual, a reenactment of a choice.

Tony's grandfather, a stonemason, came to the United States from south-ern Italy in the great migration at the start of the twentieth century. Anyone who chooses to migrate tends to carry two sets of expectations—hopes for a new life and fixed ideas from an old life. The fixed ideas that Italian immi-grants brought with them were rooted in the village life that they knew. Peo-ple lived close together, they helped each other, they intruded upon each other, they understood themselves through the eyes of these other people who formed the boundaries of their world. Interwoven networks of family and friends practiced cherished values—cooperation, loyalty, honor, and the supremacy of group interests over those of the individual.

In the New World, Italian men and women struggled to reproduce the life they remembered from the old country. They lived on the same block with people from the old village or province, they spoke the old language, they tried to live the old, premodern village life in the very cities where modernity was being born.

Whatever else organized crime may be, it is a vehicle for recreating an Italian village in a New World and preserving in the New World the old ways upon which village life had rested. By existing outside the law, an organized crime syndicate throws up invisible walls that create space for the imagined village inside the very heart of an unsuspecting modern America. Within those walls, the remembered values of the village can flourish. To those who built it, this village organization was Cosa Nostra—"our thing."

To say the least, the crime strategy was not the typical Italian American response to the dilemma of assimilation. Other choices, efforts to align middle-class American values with memories of village life were more common, but they were uneasy compromises, mixing loyalty with individualism, family with rootlessness, hierarchy with democracy. Organized crime, then, had a purity about it, a refusal to compromise, that made it visible—even riveting—for the Italian American majority that rejected its rapacity, its illegality, its apparent un-Americanism. Anyone who grew up in an Italian American community knew who the gangsters were, and many paid respect to the boss who had achieved success on his own terms.

It was the gangster's choice that Johnny Soprano made before he became the father of Tony. He opted for the honor, the pride, the loyalty, and the excitement of crime over the numbing submission of the blue-collar worker. After flirtations with mainstream American life (a failed ballplayer, a failed college student), Tony made the same choice as his father. There was a wide range of lives and identities available to Tony as a young Italian American male in postwar America, and he made the choice that was the most culturally conservative; it was, in fact, reactionary. When Tony begins each episode watching the big city recede and his neighborhood appear beyond the moat of the Meadowlands, we are reminded of the choice that he made to preserve the village and the style of manhood that flourished there.

The dilemma that confronted Tony Soprano has confronted every Italian American in some way. In the century since the great wave of immigration that swept millions of southern Italians onto America's shores, no Italian American has been able to avoid that dilemma: How Italian? How American? There has been no dominant answer to that question, but the range of answers has shaped Italian American culture and certainly Italian American manhood. The struggle between opposing cultural forces defines the essence of Italian American manhood—a struggle between the remembered manhood of premodern Italy and the manhood of modern America, between the manhood of the poor boy on the street and the manhood of the affluent American from the Ivy League. To watch Tony Soprano wage this struggle is to examine the struggle itself. The life choices of an atypical Italian American male lay bare the heart of Italian American manhood.

"I GUAGLIO": MAN AMONG MEN

One day, Tony tries to justify his life and work to his psychotherapist, Dr. Melfi, by offering a history lesson. Men like the Carnegies and the Rockefellers needed "worker bees" to "build their cities and dig their subways and make them richer." But some of the Italians who came to this country wouldn't cooperate: "Some of us didn't want to swarm around their hive and lose who we were. We wanted to stay Italian and preserve the things that meant something to us . . . honor and family and loyalty." These, then, were the cherished qualities of a man, part of an attempt to preserve what was Italian in America. It was an early and enduring interpretation of "Italian American," the pole of "Italian American manhood" that stressed the "Italian."

The village that Italian Americans of many backgrounds sought to create may or may not have been an accurate recreation of their villages in the old country. But villages—especially isolated ones—tend to share some qualities in common. People know each other well. They are often closely related. Reputations are built on intimate personal knowledge and can rise or fall with the smallest event. One's knowledge of the world is unlikely to stretch beyond the knowledge one's neighbors possess. The repository of morality is public opinion more than inner principle.

Anthropologists who have studied cultures across the Mediterranean have long recognized honor (and its inverse, shame) as keys to village life and especially to the lives of men there. As one of these scholars has written, "Honor and shame are the constant preoccupation of individuals in small scale, exclusive societies where face to face personal, as opposed to anonymous, relations are of paramount importance."[1] For some immigrant men, this older world of face-to-face contact and small scale needed to be preserved at all costs. In the midst of an anonymous and oppressive New World, a man's honor was one thing that he could preserve.

And so it was, not only in the "urban villages" inhabited by Italian American men, but also in the workplace social groups—the construction crew, the railroad gang, the factory team—where men spent so many of their waking hours. A pure version of that male "village" in America has been the world of crime created by mobsters, and the preservation of honor is at the heart of a man's life in that village. In one episode of *The Sopranos,* Christopher Moltisanti, Tony's nephew and personal aide, goes into a bakery to buy some pastry. The young man behind the counter makes Chris wait for other people who have come into the bakery after him. When Chris confronts the young man about it, the response is defiant. An argument follows, Chris pulls a gun, threatens the young man, and finally shoots him in the foot. As he leaves, Chris commands: "Next time you see my face, you better show some respect."

In any village, a man is known by his face. The face and the reputation become interchangeable. In the village maintained by gangsters, men had to keep "face." When Tony sets up his Uncle Junior to become figurehead boss after the death of Jackie Aprile, he worries to his associates, "You know, I can't be perceived to lose face." And when one of those associates, Pussy, later recalls a trivial errand on which Tony sent him, he says, "Any face I had went out the window that very day." Indeed, when Pussy later confronts his own execution, his final request is not to be shot in the face.

Face equals appearance equals reputation equals honor. A loss of honor equals shame. In a closed social world where the eyes of judgment are everywhere, shame is the most painful emotional experience. A sense of shame—a fear of it—forces people to live by the values of the group. Humiliation that is undeserved must be avenged. Thus, Chris's behavior in the bakery. Thus, the seething of Richie Aprile when the jacket he gives to Tony as a token of respect winds up on the back of the cabdriver who is married to Tony's housekeeper. Thus, the constant mobster's sensitivity about being "pissed on" or "fucked" or "spit on" by fellow members of the mobsters' village.

The shame felt by Richie, the humiliation experienced by Chris, the face lost by Pussy were all experienced in the eyes of their mobster village but could have been experienced in any of the male villages that dotted the world of Italian Americans. The likelihood of a violent response was greater among the mobsters, but the pain and humiliation may not have been greater for the majority of Italian American men who lived within the law. Pride and respect had to be maintained at all costs.

To the poor peasant, life was hard and loyalty was needed for survival. The orphaned, the crippled, and the elderly survived because others were loyal. Villages confronted with drought or epidemic relied on the fidelity of each to the other. Families in particular counted on the loyalty of their fellows. What was true for poor Italians in the old country remained true in America. And organized crime operated by a code that simply gave the basic value of loyalty an exaggerated importance.

"Old school." Over and over, Tony and his associates offer that phrase as their highest accolade. It means loyalty to one's associates, it means silence in the face of inquiries from outside the organization, or "family." As Tony explains to Dr. Melfi, "We're soldiers . . . It's war . . . We follow codes . . . orders." Theirs is a warrior ethic, and manhood within their world is wrapped up in the qualities of the warrior. The most dangerous words that one of these men can hear are the ones that Tony says to an informer as he murders him: "You took an oath and you broke it."

When Junior is taunted by federal investigators in prison who remind him of Tony's blows to his pride, Junior will not relent. He remains silent out of loyalty to Tony. When the police investigate the murder of two young toughs who tried to kill Chris, everyone remains silent, even though they know that Tony and Pussy committed the murder. Just as villagers in the old country had banded together to oppose government officials and other outsiders, so does a mobster remain loyal under pressure from "the law."

The codes and the oaths of loyalty were part of a social structure that was hierarchical. *The Sopranos* shows bureaucratic charts on FBI bulletin boards changing whenever a formal change takes place in the Mafia hierarchy. But that device is for the convenience of the viewer. Every mobster would carry a rank ordering in his head. As in a feudal order, the mobster owes fealty to those above him and noblesse oblige to those below him. He follows orders, he gives orders to those below, and he counts on the loyalty of everyone for his own survival and that of the organization. Strict social hierarchies had, of course, provided order to society in southern Italy. But of all the ordering principles of the Mob "family," this one is the least "American" and the most likely to differentiate this group of Italian American males from other kinds.

To defy the might of the government, to live outside the law, to carve out a business empire in a new and hostile environment—all these things took incredible nerve and courage. "Chutzpah," "hubris," or, in Italian, "stugots"—balls. Again, from Tony's historical explanation to Dr. Melfi: "Some of us wanted a piece of the action. We weren't educated like the Americans, but we had the balls to take what we wanted." Balls—breathtaking audacity, courage born of anger and defiance. Tony's big, showy pleasure boat is called the *Stugots*. Among Italian American men, "stugots" are generally admired. Among gangsters, "stugots" are necessary for survival.

But there are other, more subtle virtues that hold together the male sub-village—"the family"—of organized crime. Beneath the macho surface of these all-male families, there is love and affection. The men constantly exchange hugs, kisses, and pats on the cheek. And they readily verbalize this affection. Without embarrassment, Tony refers to his dying boss as a "strong, beautiful man." And he refers to Pussy as a "dear, dear friend."

Indeed, Pussy's lifelong, affectionate ties with Tony and his betrayal of those ties form one of the most poignant of *Sopranos* subplots. Pussy is an intimate member of Tony's inner circle, godfather to Tony's only son, A. J. But Pussy's heroin arrest leads him to collaborate with the FBI. Torn with anguish at having to wear "a wire" to A. J.'s confirmation and the party afterward, Pussy's grief is even greater when Tony asks him to talk sense to A. J., who is caught smoking pot during the party. Pussy goes to A. J.'s room and tells him the story of his deep, lifelong friendship with Tony, of how Tony was the only friend who showed up when his sister was dying during their teenage years. Moved by the depth and sincerity of Pussy's feelings, A. J. gets up from his bed, accepts hugs and kisses from Pussy, and goes downstairs to rejoin his family. Pussy goes into the bathroom to weep.

Once Pussy's treachery is confirmed, Tony, Pussy, and their two most intimate associates, Paulie and Silvio, head out to sea on a private boat for what they all know will be Pussy's execution. They share a round of drinks, and Paulie tells Pussy he was like a brother to him. Minutes later, Paulie and the others murder Pussy and dump his body in the ocean.

However expected, the moment is powerful because of the love among these men. Tony's dreams have been full of the pain he feels at the betrayal. And Silvio, usually seemingly without conscience about violence, leaves the room before Pussy is shot and Tony has to coax him back. The bonds of affection are deep—the betrayal is just that much more wrenching.

And the sense of family is evident at countless other points. When an assassination attempt leaves Chris's life hanging in the balance, the "family" gathers in the hospital, sharing support, comforting Chris's girlfriend, and keeping vigil until he recovers. Chris's mother appears rarely—it's clear who his true family is. Unspoken among these men as they face the possible death of a fellow is that they will die for each other. It is no accident that Italian American gangsters choose to call their organizations "families."

When business associates become one's closest friends and "family," they gain enormous social and emotional power. Fellow villagers in a threatening world, their code governs their intimate lives. In one *Sopranos'* episode, Junior's girlfriend praises his talents at oral sex, but he begs and threatens her not to tell anyone. Why? Because "they" would take his willingness to perform oral sex as a sign of weakness. Likewise, when Tony complains to Dr. Melfi that his wife thinks he should meet new people (i.e., Americans outside his criminal village), Dr. Melfi asks him what stops him. With little hesitation, he replies that "the guys" wouldn't like it.

The Italian American phrase "i guaglio" literally means, "the boys," but colloquially it is understood as a label for men in a group, for their collective behavior and customs. Among Italian American men, a night out with the "boys" is a time-honored tradition. This ordinarily means time at a club or a bar or a card game or some place deeper in the world of the male "sporting life." The tradition is not to ask the man where he's been. People in the family who talk about it will instead shrug their shoulders and say ruefully, "i guaglio."

The world of sporting life—of gambling, sex, liquor, violence—is where mobsters work, spend their time, make their money. (One of Tony Soprano's main "offices" is the Bada Bing strip club.) So occasional nights out with "the boys" are a chief point of contact between mobsters and Italian American men with legitimate jobs. Whatever feelings the average "guaglio" brings home after a night on the town, his adventures remind him of one extreme of Italian American manhood. On these nights out, a man from the mainstream can dip his toe into different waters and remind himself of a choice not made.

If the "mob life" sometimes attracts men in the mainstream, it is likely the pursuit of pleasure and the appearance of uncompromised freedom that make this life look good. But the reality of a life like Tony's constantly falls short of its own ideals. The kiss exchanged between "family" members can be the kiss of death. A hug can be obligatory or even a gesture meant to disguise dark intent. In fact, the line between affection and hostility in this world can be indistinct or completely invisible. Among friends, there is a constant flow of abusive teasing—a perpetual "cutting" contest that can erupt at any moment. Although similar to the hostile patter that is common among many kinds of Italian American men, the meanings among mobsters are more complex. The violence and anger run closer to the surface in their rough world—friendly abuse can lose its ironic edge more quickly.

When people live outside the law, their natural desire for personal safety can lead them to betray their comrades. Near the end of the first season of *The Sopranos,* it becomes clear to Tony and his associates that someone is "wearing a wire" to tape conversations for the FBI. At that point, the mistrust that never disappears in this world rises fully to the surface. Conversations, gestures, the smallest details of collegial behavior are sifted for hints of betrayal. The pervasive suspicion even infects Tony's dreams as his unconscious examines the traitorous possibilities in all of his dearest friends.

This endemic mistrust separates the criminal from the legitimate men among Italian Americans. Nor is this chronic suspicion just a matter of rational calculation in a world outside the law. Unlike most Italian American men, those in Tony Soprano's world live with their hostile, violent impulses under loose control—they know how close they are to acting on those impulses and assume that they must be likewise in danger from other men.

Moreover, in a world where anger and suspicion are facts of life, the ideals of hierarchy—of fealty and noblesse oblige—are hard to live by. The contempt of those higher in rank for those lower is rarely concealed. Tony's sneering, bullying remarks—even to his beloved if hot-headed nephew Christopher—are constant and unsparing.

The simmering tensions of hierarchy are clearest in Tony's relationship with Richie Aprile. While Richie was in jail, his brother—the boss—had died, ending the safety and the lucrative rackets that his patronage had created. Now

Richie can't get used to being a soldier out on the street, and he can't bear Tony's undisguised contempt for him. Richie's short stature is not only a symbolic gesture and a behavioral explanation—it's an excuse for the camera to look up into Tony's scornful, angry face and make us feel the humiliation of being a lowly soldier in this army. When Richie—with more "stugots" than savvy—hunts for allies in a plot on Tony's life, it's not an isolated instance. The threat of mutiny is constant. In a world that runs on honor and pride, humiliation breeds patricidal dreams. This dysfunctional "family" mixes love and abuse in ways that leave its members constantly unsettled.

"WONDERBREAD WOPS": MAN AMONG "MEDDIGAN"

The mobsters in *The Sopranos* have many audiences. There are the millions of us who watch them on TV, but within their fictional world, they have many audiences, too—the FBI and the local police; filmmakers and newscasters; puzzled, bemused colleagues in Italy; and frightened, fascinated neighbors in New Jersey. But for a consideration of Italian American manhood, the two audiences to Tony Soprano's professional world that matter most are Italian American men outside the criminal world, and Italian American women.

For the vast majority of Italian American men who live in the legitimate mainstream, their gangster brethren are like the proverbial train-wreck—they can't help but look. These men who play life by the standard American rules have made choices, too. The choices aren't as visible as the choices of Tony Soprano and his kind, because they are the expected choices, the ones that "everyone" makes. But the mainstream of Italian American men can look at mobsters and see people they may have known living out the choices that they—living a "straight" life—chose not to make. They see "the criminal element" acting out ideals that they shared on the streets and playgrounds of boyhood—freedom, adventure, "stugots," the myriad impulses that go unfulfilled in most men's daily lives but find an outlet in the life of a mobster.

The Sopranos is full of these Italian American men who left the streets for the offices, shops, and suburban homes of adult American manhood. There's Dr. Melfi's ex-husband, Richard, a bitter, deeply assimilated businessman; Davey Scatino, a high school friend of Tony's and a successful suburban sporting goods merchant with a serious gambling problem; countless FBI agents and detectives, who often look and sound like mobsters; and Father Phillip Intintola, the priest at the Sopranos' church. Father Phil is a fascinating and complex man, a shameless mooch, intellectual, thoughtful, and sensitive. But—tied in knots by his frustrated sexuality—he spends much of his energy doing fan dances of temptation with the lonely wives and widows of mobsters.

Of all these mainstream Italian American men, the two most emblematic are Tony's physician and next-door neighbor, Dr. Cusamano, and Tony's childhood friend, Artie Bucco. Dr. Cusamano is a man of easy-going charm and professional confidence. His friends (except for Dr. Melfi—he is the source of Tony's referral) are stereotypically suburban: upper-class, country-club businessmen, few of them Italian American. He does his own fan dance of temptation, but, unlike Father Phil's, his is not sexual. He is fascinated with Tony and the criminal life. He defends Tony against the scorn of his country-club friends: "Sometimes I think that the only thing separating American business from the mob is fuckin' whackin' somebody." His wife (also Italian American but even more assimilated) replies fairly: "Listen to you . . . fifteen minutes hanging around with Tony Soprano and it's 'fuckin' this and 'fuckin' that." His businessman friends, even in their disdain, are equally fascinated with the gangster in the neighborhood, and "Cus" invites Tony to play golf with them at the country club. They pump him for gangland gossip—he's there to entertain them, and their condescension can't be hidden. Tony later tells Dr. Melfi that he felt like "Jimmy Smash," a kid in school with a cleft palette who put up with the teasing of the popular kids so that he could hang around with them, but then went home and cried every night.

Cus looks a bit uncomfortable during the events on the golf course. He's a perceptive guy. And his discomfort reflects his own predicament. His friends come from the upper rungs of American suburbia, and in most ways he is one of them. But he is also Italian American and proud of his friendship with Tony.

Artie Bucco is more deeply affected by the pull between the cultures on either side of the Italian American spectrum. He is a chef who owns his own Italian restaurant. He glows with pride in his craft, and he constantly adds to his skills by learning the northern Italian cuisines that are popular with affluent Americans. He wants respect and success on American terms, and his wife,

Charmaine, wants that even more than he does. Although Artie stays on the right side of the law both as a matter of instinct and principle, he values his roots in the old neighborhood and—much to Charmaine's disgust—welcomes his mobster friends warmly to the restaurant. He is loyal to Tony, and Tony in turn showers Artie with the verbal abuse that is his way of showing affection. Artie is in fact Tony's closest friend outside of the criminal world.

But the relationship is not a simple one for Artie. Tony often calls on him for favors. When he wants help with immigration restrictions on a hit man he's importing from Italy, he asks Artie to hire him in his kitchen. And as Charmaine constantly points out to Artie, any favors that go to or from Tony are tainted with his underworld reputation and the potential for legal trouble. Artie finds himself endlessly pulled between his wife's assimilationist, upwardly mobile impulses and his friend's ethnic rootedness and illicit glamour.

Artie and Cus are two variations on the pull between "Italian" and "American" that form the central tension in Italian American manhood. They both want success and respectability on American terms, with restraint, self-discipline, delay of gratification, good taste, a comfortable income, and the material accouterments of success. But early in life they both learned a different code of manhood, based on traditional values from the old country. Mixed with that are the codes of boyhood, less distinctively of Italian descent than of the mean streets inhabited by poor people—of toughness, Darwinian struggle, self-preservation, impulsivity, and the need to gratify yourself whenever the opportunity presents itself. Artie resists but lives closer than Cus to the older world. Cus moves further toward the American way but his fascination with Tony expresses the backward pull that an upper-middle-class life can't extinguish. That mixture of Italian roots and street life pulls hard against the attraction of American life and values. No two men would resolve this dilemma in the same way, but no man in the first two generations after immigration could possibly be immune to the force of both.

Not even Tony Soprano. Tony taking his daughter to visit elite colleges; Tony worried that his son will turn out the same as he did; Tony willing to play golf with Cusamano's friends; Tony looking embarrassed when he admits to Dr. Melfi that only the bad opinion of "the guys" keeps him from socializing with "Meddigan" (Americans); Tony admitting that Americans aren't as boring as he was raised to believe. And there's Tony worrying through several episodes of the first season that his kids will find out he's a mobster.

But there's also Tony's contempt for the men who make a different choice from his. He makes his judgment of Dr. Cusamano in distinctly ethnic terms: "He's Italian but he's 'Meddigan.' He's what my old man woulda called a 'Wonderbread Wop' . . . he eats his Sunday gravy [tomato sauce] out of a jar." Running into Artie Bucco and Davey Scatino at college night at their children's high school, he says, "In high school these guys were like Joe Namath and Y. A. Tittle. Now they're like Phil Donahue and Alan Alda." His choice of mainstream men for this invidious comparison is revealing. Few entertainment figures are more closely associated with sensitive manhood than Donahue and Alda.

Tony has no patience for the psychological diagnoses and discussions of feeling that he associates with such Meddigan manhood: "It's dysfunction this and dysfunction that and dysfunction 'va fongool.'" When a school psychologist describes A. J.'s marginal ADD diagnosis, he explains that one of the symptoms is fidgeting. Tony responds that of course, he's fidgeting. He's in school all day. Besides he's going through puberty and "he gets an erection every ten minutes." And yet even in these dismissals of the psychological world of the Meddigan mainstream, Tony's own ambiguous position as a psychiatric patient is hard to avoid.

This complex conflict of manhoods appears with breathtaking surprise in the moment that Artie Bucco sticks a gun in Tony's face and threatens to shoot. Tony's mother has told Artie that Tony was responsible for the fire that burned down Artie's restaurant. The restaurant was Artie's passion and his economic support. In fact, Tony had given the order for arson, but he had done it to keep Junior from carrying out a murder there and ruining the restaurant's reputation. But he couldn't tell Artie that, so he helped Artie finance a new, bigger, fancier restaurant.

Now, as Artie looks down the barrel of his gun, one imagines his feelings about Tony. He must feel angry at Tony for destroying the business that was his pride and passion. He also carries the anger of the legitimate Italian American businessman who knows that gangsters cast a shadow of ethnic suspicion over his work. Tony also complicates Artie's marriage, because Artie and Charmaine fight constantly over Tony's influence on his life and his business. And at some level, given their common roots, he must feel some resentment at Tony for making him feel less "manly," as that word was understood in their old neighborhood.

CIVILIZATION AND ITS DISCONTENTS

Five hundred years ago in Europe, men did not settle disputes through the law or the political process. They settled them through force; whether through interpersonal violence, the clash of armies, or the threat of a prince's armed power on his subjects, it was a world where might made right. According to scholar Norbert Elias, first Western Europe and then the entire modern world underwent a "civilizing process" that changed the way people lived. The process began in the courts of France and the Italian city-states at the end of the Middle Ages. It started with a revolution in manners, making people responsible for their basic impulses—how, in public, they curbed their anger, governed their bodily functions, and controlled their sexual desires. This aspect of the process reached its culmination in the restraint that we associate with Victorian morality and the good manners of the nineteenth-century parlor. This push toward restraint went forward not through formal dictates of king or church but through emulation and social pressure, a slow but inexorable historical push in a certain direction.

As this "civilizing process" affected more and more significant individuals, its effects seeped into the lawmaking process. By the nineteenth century in many parts of Europe and North America, the state had achieved a "monopoly of violence." That is, the state had taken force out of the hands of private individuals and made itself the sole authority with power to enforce law (this in countries where the law was increasingly the creation of a democratic citizenry). In these nations, private armed forces—whether an armed gang or a prince's personal militia—were defined as threats to state, citizenry, and the rule of law.

This process of restraint and good manners coupled with the suppression of violence was a process that spread unevenly through societies. In Britain, it spread to Scotland and the north of England from the south. In the United States, it migrated from the Northeast to the South and West. And in Italy, it moved slowly southward from ancient city-states like Venice and Florence. Just as the movement of these ideals was uneven geographically, so was it uneven socially. Although these new codes of restraint began in the royal European courts, they were adopted most fiercely by the merchant class of early modern Europe. As this middle-class expanded in numbers and grew in political power, its manners and morals came to dominate society. They were "civilized" and "good," and they became markers of status and good taste.

This is emphatically not to say that regions and classes lightly affected by "the civilizing process" had no morality and no social order. It is simply to say that the codes of honor and hierarchy, of patriarchal mores and rooted loyalties and personal vengeance, that often flourished in those regions and classes were a "primitive" affront to the newer moral codes.

When millions of southern Italians and Sicilians arrived in the United States at the turn of the twentieth century, the ideals of refinement and restraint had triumphed. The new immigrants were baffled by middle-class society, and the feeling was mutual. In this historical context, disdain and puzzlement marked the relation of the new Americans to the old. Established Americans saw the new arrivals as primitive and crude—"uncivilized." And even in the second generation, as Tony Soprano notes, there were still those Italian Americans who raised their children to think of the restrained, self-denying Meddigan as "fuckin' bores."

Some of the Italian men who came to the United States found that the American code of the self-made man, with its delay of gratification and its lack of respect for tradition, fitted with their own aspirations. But others were offended by the lack of honor and loyalty and hierarchy in the new land. Some of them decided to start "their thing" and be men on terms that were familiar to them from the old country. It was these men—called "gangsters" and "hoods" by mainstream Americans—who bequeathed their values, their "families," and their village life to Johnny and Tony Soprano and other men like them.

THE TREEHOUSE AND THE FAMILY ROOM:
A MAN AMONG WOMEN

As it gained momentum into the nineteenth century, the "civilizing process" took an unexpected turn—a gendered one. Until this era, men had traditionally regarded women as less civilized than they were. Both had passions, but men had reason as a check on their passions and women didn't. Women were daughters of Eve, authors of men's temptation, more susceptible to the sins of the flesh.

But by the 1800s this view was beginning to change in the Western world, especially in northern Europe and North America. Now, men came to view women as pure, more susceptible to the movings of the Holy Spirit, and less susceptible to their own passions. In this new context, it became a woman's job to control her men's urges, to curb their impulses, to be the "civilizing" influence in the lives of husbands, fiances, brothers, and sons. The reform movements of the nineteenth century were public expressions of this impulse, as women founded and led organizations seeking to curb strong drink, prostitution, gambling, and violent pastimes such as boxing. Suddenly, the "civilizing process" had become a woman's project. This was the gender world into which Tony Soprano's grandparents entered early in the twentieth century.

In a *Sopranos* episode in which Tony is trying to explain the dangers and demands of his work to his wife, he tells her, "I took an oath." She replies, "An oath? What are you, a kid in a treehouse?" The women in Tony's life—and the wives of his associates—have much the same attitude toward Mob work and the Mob lifestyle. To them, it's childish, dangerous, and disreputable. They live with it and accept its financial rewards, but they constantly press other options on their men—home, self-restraint, the values of the Church, the standards of the larger community. The women are the "civilizing" force in these men's lives.

This division of labor and concern replicates the middle-class, Meddigan gender arrangements that dominated the nineteenth and twentieth centuries. But it also reflects the roles of mother and father that Italian Americans brought from the old country—the father was the breadwinner, the public representative, the titular head of the family; the mother raised the children, ran the household, and managed whatever finances there were to manage. In some areas of Sicily and southern Italy, the peasant father had to work far from home, and it was the mother who kept up the family's ties to its community.[2]

These gender roles rest on assumptions about sharp differences between men and women—differences that *Sopranos* characters articulate again and again. Men are driven by their urges. Some urges are harmless; when Father Phil—a self-confessed schnorrer—apologizes to Carmela for sponging yet another meal, she responds, "You're a man . . . you like to eat." But the appetite that these people most associate with men is sexual. When Tony finds that Father Phil slept at the house in his absence, he can't imagine that even a priest wouldn't try to have sex. Carmela, too, speaks of men's sexual thirst. As she helps Janice pick out a wedding dress, Carmela tells her that after a year or so she'll have to accept a "goomah" (mistress) in Richie's life. That's how it is.

Yet that's not the only general expectation of men. By nature, men are husbands and fathers responsible for their families. Tony explains his fear of a long jail term to Dr. Melfi by saying, "I just gotta stay around a little while longer for the kids." And Tony and Carmela explain his work to their kids as something he does to give them a good life. A man provides for his family.

In Tony's world, the expectations for men are split, and this split finds reflection in their behavior and feelings. Much of the behavior of Tony and his associates toward women is crude and exploitive. They rarely resist an opportunity to have sex, and they will buy it when it's not available otherwise. As soon as Tony gets comfortable with the attractive Dr. Melfi, he tries to flirt with her—that's what he brings to a relationship with a woman. And when Pussy wants to regain Tony's trust, his FBI agent advises him: "Do what you do to a girl you want to fuck. Make him love you." Tony has a goomah, a beautiful young Russian mistress with a thick accent and no other visible means of support.

The obsession of the mobsters with sex goes beyond doing it—they also profit from it. Silvio runs Bada Bing, and he and Tony are both owners. As Tony and his companions talk and do business at Bada Bing, young women—naked and amply-endowed—"dance" in the background. It's not so much a dance as a kind of joyless, unsensual slithering around a firepole. Their audience is rarely visible. And dancing is only a part of their work. The owners of the club use the "girls" to pay sexual favors to friends and associates. When Richie gets out of prison, for example, he is treated to a blow job from one of the girls.

For the men in this world, though, sex is much more complicated than pleasure or even profit. It's also a matter of power and control. In a conversation about how to run an organization, Tony reminds Junior of an old story about a father bull and his son. They're standing on a hill, looking over a field of cows, and the son says, "Dad, why don't we run down there and fuck one of these cows?" The father replies, "Son, why don't we walk down there and fuck 'em all?" At one level, this is a parable about conserving one's energy for the tasks that matter. But, more deeply, the story is about power, and the vehicle for exercising that power is sex.

And sex is not just a vehicle, it's a symbol. To be used for someone else's sexual pleasure is to acknowledge their power over you, to accept humiliation, to surrender pride. In the mobster's world, victims of the smallest slights complain of "getting fucked." Junior's oral sex problems reflect this same structure of sexual meanings. The mobsters take cunnilingus as a sign of weakness because it is a man giving pleasure to a woman, a reversal of the "proper" gender order.

Sex, then, is about the order of power, not the sharing of pleasure or the expression of love. The man who places himself below a woman threatens the superior place of every other man in the gender order. Tony can't accept that the boss in Italy is a woman. Paulie can understand Tony's going to a therapist (he's gone to one himself), but he can't accept that Tony's seeing a woman therapist. It's a blow against manhood.

Not that women, according to this view, should be powerless and contemptible. Rather, their power and status should be fully removed from their sexuality. The wives and mothers of the mobsters are placed on a pedestal, far removed from the carnality of the men's world. Their place in the world of the mobster is described by Janice (a feminist in word though not in deed). She rips into those "swaggering Mama's boy fucking hypocrites—pricks with their 'goomahs' and prostitutes . . . and they expect their wives to live like the fucking nuns of Mount Carmel College. Madonna-Whore is the full equation, I believe."

The Madonna-Whore complex operates actively in the lives of these men. Tony phones his mother from Bada Bing, with the "dancing girls" slithering naked in the background. And the plot constantly moves us from Tony with his goomah to Carmela and the Soprano household. Placing females in the gutter or on a pedestal, these men create symbolic distances between themselves and women.

But there are other ideas about women in circulation among the men. When Artie Bucco joins a party at Bada Bing to celebrate the victory of the local girls' soccer team, his discomfort is evident. He'd rather be working at his restaurant, or at home with Charmaine (viewed by the guys as a "ballbuster"). We don't know anything about Artie's sex life, but we do know that he works hard to please his wife in other ways. Tony and his friends view this behavior with scorn.

So the meanings of manhood, sex, and gender for Italian American men are multiple. Manhood can be about power—power over women, power over other men. Or it can be about intimacy and sharing—in Artie's case, sharing his food with friends, sharing power and daily life with Charmaine.

It might appear that the first option is the manly one, the "guys" option, while Artie's choice is unmanly, the one that concedes to the pressure of women. But there's something more complicated at work here. Tony's inner struggles involve many impulses, and some of them are to achieve greater intimacy—to be a better husband and a better father. There are warmly intimate sexual moments between Tony and Carmela and even moments when—usually with Carmela's prodding—he expresses the warmth and depth of his feelings for her. In one of their rare moments without anger, anxiety, or crisis, they sit quietly by the pool discussing their relationship. Carmela admits she's jealous of Dr. Melfi because she wants to be the woman in his life who can help him. He responds, "Carm, you're not just in my life. You are my life."

In a setting where men expect themselves to be eternally one-up on women, intimacy makes for complication. Intimacy means dependence and vulnerability, which in turn looks like weakness and powerlessness to many Italian American men. For all but a few, the first experience of intimacy was the first experience of powerlessness—their relation with their mother in earliest childhood.

Except for the most damaged of women (and Tony's mother Livia would fit most definitions of damaged), mothers continue to provide love, nurture, and moral guidance throughout life. But if a man is expected to be powerful and, in particular, to have power over women, then those first experiences with a woman and with intimacy pose a threat that men may spend the rest of their lives desiring and fleeing. This is the classic explanation for the Madonna-Whore complex—woman romanticized and woman demeaned. And either way, women are at a distance.

Of course, the qualities that send sons in flight from women are the very qualities that any Italian American will expect of a woman. Women are better at nurturing, says Carmela, and in that guise she tries to soften and civilize Tony. Carmela presses Tony to stick with his therapy and his anti-depressants; she urges religious faith on him and even on the impulsive Christopher as he struggles for life; she vows that she will make Tony a better father and husband.

And there are parts of this civilized ethic that Tony supports passionately. He wants his home to be a safe haven for his wife and children, a gated castle. He wants his children sheltered from the violence, carnality, and double-dealing of his own world. One night, when the subject of sex comes up at the dinner table, Tony shouts, "Maybe it's the 1990s out there, but in here it's 1954!" Ironically, Tony wants to provide his children with protection from men like himself, from the impulses he knows he can barely control.

If Tony feels like his children need to be protected against his kind, it's not surprising that he seems awkward as a father. When he wants to have a candid talk with Meadow or A. J., he always chooses the wrong moment. And in a parenting crisis, it's Carmela who takes control. For example, when Meadow throws a wild party at her grandmother's empty house and one friend goes to the hospital with an overdose, it's Carmela who yells out the punishments and parries Meadow's adolescent excuses. Tony stands in the background shouting, "Yeah, that's right!"

Tony is less comfortable at home with Carmela and the kids than he is with the guaglio. In one episode, Tony has been advised by his lawyer to stay away from his associates, so he hangs around the house. Bored and restless, he gets up late and wanders past Carmela's reading group in his bathrobe. At the end of the episode, he returns to his "office" at the back of Satriale's, where he finds contentment with his other family. A quiet card game goes on, Tony buffs his shoes, Paulie stands at the stove, cooking and murmuring to Silvio about skin lotions and suntans. This peaceful domestic tableau looks for all the world like the standard Victorian parlor portrait, with family members amusing themselves and each other in quiet, unspoken affection.

The men in Tony's world deeply need this comfort zone. Indeed, one of the ironies of their situation is that, as much as they choose a life of danger, they spend much of their energy defending their bastions of security—their families, their social and professional villages. It's the women in their lives who branch out, who build bridges to the rest of the Italian American community and to the larger, middle-class world of the Meddigan. Carmela, for instance, is a walking encyclopedia of assimilation. She quotes *Time* magazine on father-son relationships, introduces the bourgeois injunction against violence into Soprano child-rearing, builds networks in the community, and tends to the family's social status. When she decides to have a fundraiser for the local hospital at their house, Tony whines, "Since when do we open our house to strangers?" Carmela confronts his fearfulness: "What do you wanna do? Go back to the Middle Ages and build a castle and a moat and pour hot oil on anybody that tries to get in?" In fact, this is a description of stunning precision—not just of Tony's worldview but of the village mentality that animates his professional world.

Tony, of course, would say that he is animated by ethnic pride, and he would be right. But that wouldn't make Carmela's interpretation wrong. In fact, one of the complications in the dynamic of Italian American manhood is that it's not clear who's fearful and who has "stugots." Certainly, Tony leads a more adventurous life than Artie or Dr. Cusamano, taking more risks in a day than they might take in a month. But they have also taken risks—risks that make Tony cringe with fear. They have long since waded into the alien world of the Meddigan, adjusted to new ways, worked to find the best of both worlds for themselves and their families. Which is the strong and brave choice? Which is manly and which is unmanly? The standard answer would favor Tony's romantic, defiant choice. The truth is far more complicated.

Likewise, Carmela's position between Italian and Meddigan worlds is complicated. Within the circle of mobster wives, she is a traditionalist. When Pussy's wife, Angie, decides to get a divorce, Carmela urges forbearance. Marriage, she says repeatedly, is a holy sacrament. The family is a sacred institution. She worries that Pussy and Angie's kids will be "fatherless children from a broken home" if the divorce goes through. Angie's intentions are so threatening to Carmela that she seems oblivious to her friend's pain. Tony and Carmela may disagree on many cultural issues, but this is one that unites them in opposition to the suburban mainstream flowsing around them.

In fact, this is one issue on which the mainstream itself has shifted course. Not even the Meddigan spoke easily of divorce when Carmela and Tony's ancestors came from the old country a century ago. With the passage of time, some Italian Americans adopted the dominant American values even as those values flowed further and further from the course of premodern traditionalism. Indeed, the real villains in Tony's world are not so much American values and institutions as they are time and change.

"THE BEST IS OVER":
MANHOOD AND HISTORICAL CHANGE

In the opening scene of the first episode of *The Sopranos,* Tony and Dr. Melfi explore the feelings that have precipitated his panic attacks. What he describes are feelings of loss and decay. He says that he has come in at the end of something—something for which his father laid the ground floor. He envies his father the heroic opportunity to found something, to live in a time of pride and high standards. Although Tony's father "never reached the heights like me," Tony feels like a lesser man, doing what he can to preserve an enterprise in decline.

The immediate event, though, that had precipitated his first panic attack was the departure of a family of ducks from the swimming pool in his backyard. The ducks had become an obsession to Tony in the weeks before their departure. He fed them, he talked to them, he built a ramp into the pool for the babies, he kept a book about birds close at hand. It moved Tony deeply that these wild creatures came to his pool to have their babies. When they left, he collapsed.

Feelings of loss permeate Tony's life. And, given his definition of his life, Tony's grief is inevitable. He understands his life as a form of resistance to American culture. He wants to maintain the values of his Italian ancestors, he wants to recreate an Italian village that preserves timeless values and customs, that reveres tradition and resists change.

This ancient village that Tony struggles to preserve exists in his imagination. Even in its premodern state, it was never changeless.[3] And surely changelessness cannot be achieved in a nation whose first principle is change. The Italian ideal was that the son should emulate the father and respect him. The American ideal is that the son should surpass the father and leave him. Tony's dream is doomed.

Tony and his associates constantly lament the passing of the standards on which their code of manhood is based. Pussy describes it with vehemence: "Like Tony says, there's no fucking honor any more. Forget your enemies, you can't even depend on your friends." As if to prove his point, Pussy's audience for this denunciation is the federal agent to whom he is betraying Tony. Gone with loyalty and honor are respect for one's superiors and for the principles of hierarchy that make them superior. Ambitious though he is, young

Christopher shows up for work when he feels like it and carries out executions and hijackings without consulting Tony.

And whatever reverence for family that may once have existed has vanished. Tony's mother encourages Junior to kill Tony. Junior gives the order. Tony tries to kill his mother and orders the execution of Junior. The murders never happen, but the intent eats away at Tony and at Junior, too. The personal betrayal here is devastating, but these homicidal rages also attack the fundamental principle of family on which these men have staked their integrity.

But it's not only the standards of manhood that are in decline. It's the men themselves. When Tony looks at his father, he sees a pioneer, a man who knew what he wanted to do and did it. Although he's aware of his father's shortcomings, he admires his father's certainty and his fidelity to principle—and he contrasts that with his own doubts and failures.

Then he looks at his son A. J. and sees proof that the old manhood is dying out. In his early adolescence, A. J. is not a "guy's guy," and he's clumsy when he tries to be—he's the kind of kid who always gets caught. Neither a street kid nor an extracurricular whiz, A. J. likes to watch TV and play video games. None of this escapes Tony's notice. While Carmela is campaigning for Tony to get a vasectomy, A. J. leaves the TV long enough to get a high-calorie snack and breaks a dish in the process. Tony turns to Carmela and says, "I'm supposed to get a vasectomy when this is my male heir?" In a moment of greater sympathy, Tony worries to Carmela that A. J. has no street smarts, that he needs to toughen up and not be a sucker. There are no signs that A. J. will turn out to be much of anything, and he certainly has none of his grandfather's daring energy—no stugots.

In his own life and in the son he has produced, Tony feels like he has failed to maintain what his father started. And there is another generational promise that Tony hasn't kept. Tony believes that a man takes care of his mother when she can no longer take care of herself. But Livia Soprano is not a sweet old lady. She refuses to be cared for and rejects even the smallest gestures of help. Tony is the only sibling who keeps trying to help his mother, and he is wracked with guilt when he puts her in an assisted living facility. In fact, his second anxiety attack hits him during a preadmission visit to the place. He has become a symbol to himself of manhood in decline.

To make matters worse for Tony, his premodern ideas about manhood have to compete with a postmodern flood of information. Some of the male images in the media make sense to Tony: the soldiers on the History Channel, Gary Cooper and his silent stoicism, the *Godfather* movies. But the cultural politics of modern American gender are far more complicated than that, and they pour through the media and through daily conversation. Even the mobsters who haven't seen a psychiatrist can speak in the language of popular psychology. Richie Aprile learns yoga in prison and can talk in a New Age argot of sensitivity with Tony's sister Janice (who during one residence in a commune changed her first name to Parvati). Father Phil plies Carmela with a new generation of Catholicism that includes art films and books on Buddhism. The fight between Richie and Janice that leads to Richie's murder starts with an argument about what it means that Richie's son is gay. And certainly Carmela's bourgeois ideas about vasectomy contradict Tony's ideals of manhood.

Of all the new American ideas about gender, feminism looms especially large. Allying itself with psychology, it supports a larger domestic role for men. Sharing principles with New Age thought, it urges men to be more expressive of tender feelings. Speaking from its own political core, it demands an equality between the sexes that flatly contradicts the dominance that men like Tony expect in their relationships with women.

And yet, this constant flow of contrary ideas and images may not even be the single greatest threat to the code of manliness that Tony and his friends hold sacred. The greatest danger is the core ideal of American manhood—independence. To be sure, the ideal espoused by the mobsters respects the possibilities of individual courage and achievement, but those accomplishments are understood in a context of deep interdependence. Consider the values that Tony says organized crime meant to preserve: honor, family, and loyalty. Each is a value about the proper relation of each man to the other. The very essence of the organized crime "family" is that a man submerges his personal well-being in the well-being of the group.

Tony's worldview carries the suspicion of independence even further than that. The village that Tony seeks to recreate in his organization and in his mind reveres tradition and never changes. Families stay together and each generation picks up the destiny of the one before. Tony's belief in the shared fate of generations comes out clearly in a debate with Dr. Melfi about free will and determinism. A. J. has been misbehaving at school and is being tested for ADD, and a wave of memories suddenly floods through Tony's daily life—memories of his own childhood and his own father. He tries to sort out the meaning in Dr. Melfi's office: "Me . . . my father . . . it's probably in the genes, right?" His ambivalence about living outside the law and his worries about his panic attacks crowd him. He asks Dr. Melfi, "My son is doomed, right?" adding, "I don't want him to be like me." She replies that people have choices, then asks in wonderment if he thinks everything is preordained. His reply is unhesitating: "You're born to this shit, you are what you are."

This kind of fatalism has often characterized traditional cultures and certainly influenced many Italian immigrants in America. In his warm, evocative memoir of Sicilian family life in Rochester, New York, Jerre Mangione places *destino* squarely at the center of his parents' understanding: "'E u destino.' That single phrase explained everything. 'The good Lord has decided in advance what is going to happen to all of us. You can't fight Destiny,' my mother would often say to me."[4] The dark certainty of the parents' outlook casts a large shadow over their American-born children:

> To us [children] *destino* never seemed to have any connection with God. Hell appeared like a more likely place for it. It hung over our thoughts like an unassailable dragon who somehow had become the final authority in determining the outcome of all important happenings in our lives, regardless of what our teachers and the Horatio Alger novels said to the contrary.[5]

Not even the pervasive American culture could erase the shadow of *destino* from the lives of these Italian American children.

That is unquestionably the case for Tony. He's convinced that the modern, scientific version of *destino* ("it's probably in the genes") has determined his fate and that of his son. Dr. Melfi is incredulous. After all, she had to believe in her ability to mold her own fate in order to make a life in America's professional class. She says passionately, "You have a range of choices. This is America." To which Tony can only reply with a caustic, "America . . . right." Tony may be the head of a large organization, making command decisions all day long, but he doesn't for a moment believe that his life is in his own hands. In that, he refuses to accept the most basic tenet of American manhood.

And yet he can't resist the desire for his kids to be successful on America's terms, and that's what's pulling him apart. His children are about to leave the nest in American fashion. On the day that the flight of the ducks precipitates his first panic attack, Meadow and Carmela are fighting about Meadow's proposed ski trip to Aspen with her best friend. A senior in high school, she is desperate to put a continent between herself and her parents by going to college in California. Her parents don't want her that far away, and yet they do want her to go to a high-status private college. Perhaps the most famous of all *Sopranos* episodes is the one in which Tony leaves Meadow by herself for a day at Colby College, while he goes off to murder a man with his bare hands—for breaking a traditional oath of loyalty. Meadow swims independently in the mainstream as Tony retreats to the murky waters of an ancient code. Ultimately, Meadow achieves the success for which Tony hopes, entering Columbia (high in status and close to home). But culturally Columbia is thousands of miles from Tony's village. It's full of strangers, and one of them (half-Black, half-Jewish) becomes Meadow's boyfriend. Tony's rage is as predictable as it is helpless.

Tony's inability to keep his own children in his village reflects a larger trend. Starting with the generation born in the 1930s, the majority of Italian Americans with two Italian American parents married non–Italian American spouses. As the decades have passed, the percentage of outmarriage has increased. This means that most Italian American children are only partly so, and the "dilution" of ethnicity grows with every passing year of deaths, marriages, and births. Italianness becomes a memory more than a commitment. Tony's ethnic struggle is quixotic, as the old values and the old manhood fade in what one scholar has called the "twilight" of Italian American ethnicity. Tony and his generation of mobsters are raising a generation of TV-watching, mall-going, private-college-attending suburbanites. In the adulthood of those children, there will be even fewer Tonys, more Artie Buccos and Dr. Cusamanos, and a growing number who will have little sense of their ethnicity at all.

THE CULT OF FRANCIS ALBERT: MANHOOD AT THE TURN OF THE TWENTY-FIRST CENTURY

The Sopranos are sitting around the table, eating take-out, when Tony launches into a lesson on ethnic pride. He and Carmela review the great accomplishments of Italians through the centuries. From da Vinci to Enrico Fermi, the list is a long one. Finally, they arrive at a great Italian whose name can't be topped. "Francis Albert," says Tony with a proud grin and a knowing glance at his wife. End of discussion.

To anyone growing up in an Italian American household in the decades after World War II, Frank Sinatra was a familiar topic of discussion. Italian Americans viewed him with a mixture of reverence and fascination. He was the most successful Italian American entertainer of his generation—a popular, critically acclaimed, enormously well-paid singer and an Oscar-winning actor. But his fascination to his fellow "paesans" went well beyond his professional success. His attraction had to do with his insouciant attitude, his disdain for the conventions of the entertainment world and of polite society. "Frankie" (as he was familiarly known to my relatives) was unabashedly Italian, from the cut of his suits to the unchanged vowel at the end of his name. The arrogant cool of his persona reflected (and ultimately must have influenced) the image of the gangster. He would get what he wanted and he would get it on his own terms. If he wanted to hang out with Mob bosses, he would—and if presidents wanted to be his friend, they would have to take him as he was, ethnic style, mobster friends, and all. He would be true to his people and to their code—and for this Italian Americans loved him.

To put this another way, Frank Sinatra's transcendent appeal to Italian Americans had little to do with the intimate, sublimely phrased recordings from the 50s that have endeared him to jazz critics. It had everything to do with the Rat Pack ethos, with Vegas and fist fights with reporters and a dream world of money and power taken on one's own terms. If there were a theme song for the cult of Francis Albert, it wouldn't be "One for My Baby" or "In the Wee Small Hours," it would be "(I Did It) My Way."

He is an expression of Tony Soprano's ideal of manhood—keeping the Italian values but grabbing a piece of the American action. But where Tony and others like him have to go outside the law to achieve these two goals, Sinatra did it all legally, did it all in public view, and even (at least artistically) did it with the approval of the mainstream American audience. He did it his way—and he had it both ways.

If Frank Sinatra was a successful Italian American man on both ends of the spectrum, Tony himself would be scorned by most Americans (perhaps even by most Italian Americans) if he were a real person. He works outside the law, he lives by violence, and he promotes corruption and vice. Tony would be a role model to very few Italian American boys. He doesn't even want his own son to turn out like he is.

And yet the meaning of his life and of his manhood has an ironic Americanness. He and the mobsters who came before him showed a stunningly American impatience with the slow, arduous paths of upward mobility. Tony's cunning, wit, energy, nerve, initiative, and extraordinary understanding of the markets he serves make him in many ways a model entrepreneur. So, as repugnant as Tony's style is to American values (and that's how he wants it), he is also a successful American businessman.

There are two ways to end this chapter. One is eulogistic. Italian American manhood is in its twilight because Italian Americanness itself is fading. Certainly, there are still neighborhoods where Italian Americans intermarry and where the sights and the smells and the sounds of Italian America fill the air. But the sojourners of the great migration are long gone. The ties to the old country have faded and even the myths of "the village" that began with the immigrants themselves have grown dim (can we imagine A. J. waxing eloquent about Italian values at freshman football practice?). And if your father is a half or a quarter Italian, what does Italian American manhood mean to you anyway? Tony may aspire to be like Gary Cooper in *High Noon,* but he's more like the last of the Mohicans. And he knows it.

But ethnic values and ethnic manhood are not just a lived experience that belong to a group. They are images that express values, and like any image they are available to anyone who encounters them, inside the group or out. And here is a different sort of ending.

Post-Reagan America—the America of deregulation and the heroic entrepreneur—has seen a rebirth of the symbols of the Sinatra era. The cocktail, the cigar, the gambling casino (the revenge of the Mohicans?) and even *Ocean's Eleven* are all back for another spin. You don't hear "One for My Baby" any more, but "My Way" has found a second life at cocktail lounges and karaoke nights across America. The Sinatra image fits the era of the brash entrepreneur. The 80s and 90s nurtured a code of manhood that honored boldness and defiant ambition—stugots.

That sounds like Tony Soprano. He's a shrewd operator, a man with a brilliant eye for the main chance, a man who stays on top in a turbulent business—and a man who indulges in America's illicit love affair with violence.

He delivers an Italian American manhood that is ready-made, a staple of American culture retooled for a new era.

And at one level, that's true. Tony stands for a kind of "My Way" manhood, tailored for the turn of the twenty-first century. But *The Sopranos* would not be an award-winning and critically acclaimed phenomenon if it were simply another rewarming of old gangster myths. There's something far more complex going on in the show and in the images of manhood that it presents.

Tony and the men around him are complex individuals, their swagger and their violence qualified by doubts and fears. Tony in particular has a rich, fascinating, and painful inner life. He is a real man—not "real" in the sense of ideal but "real" in the sense of fully and authentically human. *The Sopranos* also lifts Italian American manhood out of the gangster myth through its female characters. It gives as much humanity to its women as to its men, and it lets us see the pull that Italian American women have always exerted on their men. Then, too, *The Sopranos* shows us a variety of Italian American men outside the Mob—Father Phil and Dr. Cusamano and (especially and respectfully) Artie Bucco. Finally, *The Sopranos* gives us values such as loyalty, rootedness, and interdependence—values that have provided a foundation for Italian American manhood and offered common manly ground to the Artie Buccos and the Tony Sopranos. Part of Tony's humanity—and part of his tragedy—is that he knows America (whatever its common pieties) is hostile to those values. He believes in his soul that those values—and not gunplay—are what Italian American men could have brought to American culture. He wants to bring those values back, but he knows that, like his ducks, they will not return.

THE CULTURAL WORK OF
THE SOPRANOS

Jay Parini

The Sopranos is important because it interrogates American culture at the turn of this century with a ruthlessness rarely seen on television, at least in a country like the United States, where television producers have normally run away from serious commentary. This is a large series, with many threads, all woven in interesting and complex ways. I will address only a few of them, although I marvel at the richness of the whole.

One aspect of the series I will consider only briefly is its relationship to Italian American culture. The question that arises usually runs along these lines: Does *The Sopranos* represent just another negative portrayal of Italian Americans? One is used to seeing Italian Americans cast as thugs and gangsters in the movies, and *The Godfather* series—however brilliant and entertaining—seems only the most obvious example of this tendency. I don't think there is any doubt that *The Sopranos* rather nakedly trades on this stereotype of Italian American culture. The series does nothing to represent Italian Americans as they truly are: a diverse cultural strand in American society that has its share of thugs but also has a generous share of economists, scientists, writers, filmmakers, and political leaders. American business culture would be impoverished if the Italian American strain were removed from its history. This point is obvious and almost beside the point.

The Sopranos may well do some damage to the image of Italian Americans. It reinforces stereotypes, of course, and that is always a bad thing. More damagingly, perhaps, it seduces Italian Americans to invite these stereotypes, thus reinforcing a sense of self that has already been projected onto them by the media. Life imitates art as much as the other way around, as the writers of *The Sopranos* obviously know, and satirize in the scenes where the Soprano gang are clearly acting in imitation of the *Godfather* films. But the further point is that the Italian American community may well act out the stereotypes handed them so easily. That is how stereotypes function.

These negative aspects of the series don't stop it from being a work of art in itself. For me, *The Sopranos* represents an intriguing and significant interrogation of American society as a whole, and Italian Americans (such as myself) will have to put up with the image-related problems or confront them elsewhere. What fascinates me is the way the series walks a desperately thin line between realism and satire.

Tony Soprano is, for the most part, a fairly realistic character, especially as played by James Gandolfini, who embodies this character with unusual subtlety. Tony is someone we meet on the street every day in the United States: the genial, temperamental, unpredictable, depressed American male. That he is also a ruthless killer does not surprise us, partly because Gandolfini makes the transition from neurotic husband and father to ruthless criminal boss so seamlessly, and partly because we now accept violence as part of everyday life. Watching the evening news, we can't get away from it, even if it doesn't happen to play out before our eyes on the street.

Dare I say it? I personally identify with Tony Soprano, as I suspect many American men do. While the material circumstances of Tony's life and mine could not be more different, when I'm watching the program, I find myself "identifying" in the old-fashioned way. His anxiety attacks, problems with his kids, troubles at work, and so forth, feel horribly familiar. Anxiety is so much a part of contemporary culture that we take it for granted, and it's extremely useful to see the problems we all face—mobsters and the rest of us—played out in such vivid, often comical, ways. There is even a sense of relief in seeing that a powerful mobster, a man of considerable resources like Tony Soprano, is prey to the same issues.

Tony suffers, without quite knowing it, the guilt that attends us all. His anxieties are, of course, rooted in his unique professional situation: He might get nabbed by the Feds at any moment, locked up for life, even fried in the chair. His friends and family are perpetually threatened by extinction. This sort of thing would make anyone nervous; but part of the charm of the series lies in the fact that—in addition to his professional problems—Tony worries as well about what college his daughter, Meadow, will attend. He frets about the circumstances of his son, Anthony, Jr.—who seems on the verge of turning into a thug like his father. He worries about his mother, Livia Soprano, in a way that must seem typical to many Americans of a certain age. He is having trouble with his sexuality and trouble with money. It's not so hard to "identify" with all of this. I suspect that millions do.

But what *The Sopranos* makes clear with the devastating force of its satire is that a lot of our anxieties that seem strictly personal are standing in for deeper social and moral anxieties. Tony's world is built on a series of crimes. Brutality, extortion, and murder are everyday stuff for the Mob. Tony's high standard of living—the large suburban house, its swimming pool and patio, the gadget-filled kitchen—depends upon these ugly but hidden crimes. He only dimly knows this, yet the guilt of it plagues him, coming out in odd and unexpected ways. In a very real sense, Tony's situation mirrors that of all Americans.

Our great wealth as a nation is founded on brutality, extortion, and murder. This sounds exaggerated, put so bluntly, but isn't it true? In historical time, it really isn't so long ago that European invaders appropriated an entire continent from Native Americans. Millions were killed in that westward expansion, sacrificed in our belief that (as Robert Frost put it) "The land was ours before we were the land's." Soon slaves were imported from Africa to perform the hard agricultural labor that the white population could not manage—or didn't want to manage. Millions—one estimate puts the number at sixty million—died as a direct result of the institution of slavery. This was not a long time ago: my own great-grandfather fought in the Civil War, and I used to hear about his exploits from my grandfather, who was born in 1892.

The American empire has reached to every continent, and our immense wealth is uncomfortably perched on our exploitation of resources that we have wrested from people who are too weak to prevent us from acting in this bullying way (a manner perfected by Tony Soprano in his capo mode). In most cases, we have paid somebody for their raw materials, but we have often just enriched a tiny group in the country—the elite who happens to control those resources. The oil of the Middle East is a fine example. A few sheiks—in Saudi Arabia, the House of Saud itself—control this valuable resource, which would in a more reasonable world belong to the people of the region, who remain in relative poverty. That many of them feel extremely angry about this situation should come as no surprise.

One could go on. The story of our exploitation of South America and Central America is a long, sad, and well-documented tale, and there seems no end of it. Even the threat to the environment posed by the destruction of rain forests seems to upset only those on the so-called lunatic fringe (vast tracts of open land are apparently required for cattle grazing so that cheap hamburgers can be sold at McDonalds). The sordid history of fruit and coffee production—to say nothing of the story of cocaine, the supply of which is rarely interrupted, except once in a while to demonstrate the effectiveness of the War on Drugs—has been written and ignored.

Now most of the products we depend on each day, from apparel to furniture, electronics equipment to building materials like steel, are manufactured abroad, in sweatshops. It's no secret that women and children are ruthlessly exploited in these factories, in Indonesia, Malaysia, Southeast Asia, and elsewhere. Their arduous labor and excruciating poverty make possible our ease and improbable wealth.

Most of us know this, but we suppress the knowledge in order to survive. We may believe we're dependent on cheap oil, cheap clothing, and cheap food. Yet we secretly suspect that we should not be enjoying ourselves so much, living so grandly, so wildly above our means. There should be more justice in the world. But there is not, and we inevitably play a role in this imbalance. Like Carmela, we try to compensate for this imbalance by giving to charitable causes and doing good works; sometimes we even pray. But our efforts seem ineffectual, minimal, and futile; they eventually drive us crazy.

The Soprano family stands in for all of us here. They live high off the hog in a glitzy suburban home, a parody of the American dream, resplendent with all the gadgets and appliances that make living easy. There is a microwave oven, an array of high-tech kitchen appliances, a vast freezer full of prepared foods, air-conditioning, and so forth—everything readily at hand for Meadow and her friend, Hunter, as they feast while doing homework. There is a heated swimming pool and a grill in the backyard. Everyone has a car. Meadow, in one episode, inherits the SUV formerly driven by her best friend at school—the vehicle given to Tony in partial payment of debts acquired by the friend's father in a night of gambling with the Soprano gang. (This moment in the series makes explicit the usually covert trope of illegitimate appropriation.) In miniature, this is the American dream, and it's not really so different from what goes on in many neighborhoods around the country.

The Sopranos are not only stereotypical; they are archetypal, almost paradoxically so. Indeed, the screenwriters appear to delight in playing with this aspect of the drama. Carmela—superbly played by Edie Falco—represents the stereotypical suburban housewife and mother. Appearances are everything to her. She is never satisfied, materially or sexually, and is always on the verge of an affair: with the local priest, with the wallpaper hanger. That her husband is having affairs with whores seems to bother her only when her lifestyle is otherwise threatened. Meadow stands in for the teenage daughter from Hell: chewing gum, listening to rock at a decibel level designed to inflict maximum damage on any eardrum within a hundred feet, perfecting her skills as an artful dodger of responsibilities, trying to get ahead in life by whatever means are available. The writers, who once again demonstrate their acute understanding of the suburban teenage scene, neatly evoke her world.

The episodes in which Carmela sets to work to get Meadow into Georgetown University by eliciting a recommendation from the sister of her neighbor is priceless: only a slight parody of what actually goes on in families around the country when their kids are applying to colleges. The fact that Tony Soprano has the clout to do serious physical damage to the woman if she won't write the letter of recommendation simply makes a trope explicit that is usually covert. The scene in which Carmela actually visits the office of the woman-of-influence operates, parodically, on many levels: the fact that this is a woman visiting a woman is in itself vaguely satirical, since one associates this sort of ritual with a man's world. American society—especially in its business and political realms—runs on favors, on influence, although influence is usually wielded quietly, behind the boardroom door. But pressure of one kind or another is commonly brought to bear, and the Mafia's coercive methods simply fall on the most explicit side of what must be considered a spectrum. It is both funny and eerie to watch Carmela playing out the ritual so explicitly, and becoming in the course of the series more like Tony and his crew, adopting their methods and values. (Of course the relation-ships among members of the Mafia gang also parody "normal" business rela-tions. Indeed, since the business of America is business, what most vividly occurs while watching the Sopranos making their deals is that what they're involved in seems rather ordinary.)

Tony himself is the most archetypal character in the pack. The splits in his life are typical of what many American men experience, although exag-gerated to the point of satire. The sexism that is gaudily on display at the Bada Bing Club, with nude dancers constantly on the stage (it's always mid-night in the bar) and whores giving blow jobs in the back room (one involv-ing Richie getting a blow job while he is talking to someone else about business), reminds us that women often "perform" on the fringe, in positions where their exploitation is taken for granted. Women in the Mob are bla-tantly ornaments, toys, and temporary distractions. Their chief function is to pump up the male ego, and to satisfy the male wish for sexual gratification without emotional contact. Feminist critics have long ago covered this ground, but what *The Sopranos* does so beautifully is to remind us that noth-ing has changed for most women in the world.

The series reminds us of this by calling attention to the problem of sex-ism in an exaggerated form. In fact, the exaggerations are not so extreme. In the largely ethnic community where I was raised, the attitudes represented by the world of the Bada Bing Club were commonly on view. A lot of men acted pretty much like Tony and his friends—or adopted an attitude that would not have been unfamiliar in the Bada Bing. Women in the home, of course, were treated as sacred objects, to an extent; the famous virgin/whore dichotomy was firmly in place, and a woman fell into one category or an-other. Doubtless the crass, unapologetic mistreatment of women that one sees in *The Sopranos* is an exaggeration, in its brutality and explicitness; but it serves to point a finger at lesser but still horrendous injustices that not only linger in but pervade American culture.

Once again, *The Sopranos* succeeds by taking what is "normal" and exag-gerating it; it draws attention to the fault lines in family and community life, and it makes overt what is usually covert. It plays with stereotypes, winking at us as it does so, treading a line between realism and fantasy. Its distortions are almost believable, as in the character of Tony's mother, one of the most vivid creatures in the extended Soprano family.

If Tony Soprano is Everyman writ large, Livia Soprano (so remorselessly captured by the late Nancy Marchand) is Everyman's Mother. She embodies all aspects of the narcissistic mother, and her dialogue is pitch perfect as she mocks, derides, scorns, and casts aspersions upon all around her. Nobody is good enough for her except, perhaps, her deceased husband, who was "a saint," as she reminds us endlessly. Indeed, "Your father was a saint" is her mantra, used to quiet the waters around her. A saint who just happens to have been a master thief, extortionist, and cold-blooded murderer. Alas, Tony must live up to this role model, and the strain shows; he isn't cut out for the job, emotionally, having been hobbled by his mother, who must spend all her time nursing her own narcissistic wound.

A narcissist is not just a self-centered person; it is also someone who has an inordinate need to have the world reflect his or her emotional shifts. Since the world rarely complies, the narcissist distorts what is happening, seeing everything that occurs in his or her own special terms. Selfishness is only the most obvious element in the narcissistic personality. There is often a ruthlessness on display, too, and a desire to kill everything or everyone who does not share in the narcissist's private dream. In most cases, the narcissism in question is not so extreme as in the personality of Livia Soprano, who *literally* attempts to kill her son. But the archetype is useful here in making everything so clear, so explicit, so perfectly realized. Nancy Marchand, with every gesture and inflection, summons a world of brutal egotism, resentment, and stifling anger.

She also represents a generational dividing line. Only Corrado Soprano, Uncle Junior, knows the truth about her generation, has gone through the same conflicts—the Depression, the war—and understands her world with any real intimacy. They are a bizarre couple, thrown together by loneliness and need, and their meetings are always rather touching. Neither of them can understand the next generation, represented by Tony. They both would like Tony dead, and since the means for getting rid of people are rather too available, it follows that murderous thoughts should give way to attempted murder.

Livia Soprano has been nicely schooled in ruthlessness, and she will stop at nothing to get what she wants. It requires little imagination to suspect that Tony was subjected to her violent whims from an early age. His own fragile ego was formed in her shadow, and he is only in late middle age beginning to feel the full brunt of his rage. He is royally pissed, and his mother is getting from him what he believes she deserves. (That Livia so passionately resents her son's attitude is also quite believable: she has not been used to having her hand called.)

There are problems with this, of course. On the one hand, Tony insufficiently understands what is happening between himself and his mother. His rage against her seems to have come from nowhere, and he is terrified by it. It contributes to his overall anxiety, adding to the level of tension that lies behind his anxiety attacks. On the other hand, he fails to understand where his mother might be coming from. What can it have been like for her to have been married to the Mob? She spent her adult life terrified that her husband would be wiped out or jailed. There can have been very little emotional security in the Soprano nuclear family.

Crime pays, but the proceeds are unreliable. And there are endless, unforeseen consequences for everyone connected to the family. Mobsters supposedly revere motherhood, and wives and children are spared the violence that the male members of the clan must confront on a daily basis. This theme is a staple of Mob fiction; it runs through the *Godfather* movies, even through *Goodfellas.* But in "real life," the women do get hurt, at least emotionally. They often get hurt physically as well. There is abuse everywhere in the Mob family circle, and women are spared in theory only.

Livia Soprano is one of the most pathetic characters in the series: a wounded, self-hating, helpless, vicious, miserable creature who has managed to isolate herself from the world at great cost. She sighs and moans, and her voice is full of pain and anger. She lashes out at anyone who comes near, even those who might help in some way.

Tony's dilemma seems typical of men of his life stage. What is one to do with one's elderly mother? Is assisted living really a form of Hell? Can one put the person who brought you into the world and raised you into a situation she detests, at the end of life? How much time is one to spend with one's mother in her last years? To what extent does one write off the past? Who foots the bills? The questions multiply in Tony's head as they do in the heads of every fifty-something child with a widowed mother in uncertain health. Once again, the brilliance of this series turns on the way it takes a very ordinary problem and blows it up, makes it garishly colorful but hideously real. One would hate to imagine the number of male viewers in America who studied the antics of Livia Soprano and, under their breath, whispered to themselves, "Mom!"

America's obsession with psychotherapy is another aspect of life that *The Sopranos* confronts with a kind of malicious glee. Dr. Jennifer Melfi is among the most fetching creations of the series, wonderfully acted by Lorraine Bracco. One hears that therapists across the country find her riveting, and no wonder. She seems professional to a hilt, especially in the early programs, in her neat suits and serious glasses, with her sympathetic gaze that never quite lets go of its moral neutrality. When Tony accuses her of passing judgment on his sex-life, she bridles, insisting that she would never pass judgment on a patient's sexual behavior. That's just not kosher. An analyst in America today is a secular priest, and she does not make value judgments. She is there to help the patient understand the relationship between his past and present, to help integrate his personality, and to relieve the symptoms of his distress by passing out the appropriate medication and by giving him access to the "talking cure."

Once again, the writers of *The Sopranos* appear to have been gifted with perfect pitch, and the scenes in the therapy sessions are brilliantly choreographed. Tony's posture, his expressions, his gesticulations, all seem real. Dr. Melfi assumes the perfect guise of the disinterested analyst, crossing her legs to contain herself, looking at Tony over the rims of her glasses on a few occasions, to suggest that she just might break through the professional decorum. Her body language is remarkably well choreographed, allowing her to maintain absolute neutrality. That Tony is a murderer, a thief, and a serial adulterer is not relevant to her work; she must try to keep her sense of decorum, her "professional" cool.

Therapists have, it often seems, taken over the role of priest in the contemporary world of middle-class American. The "real" priests are tainted, as we have seen with Carmela's own priest, who uses his role to play his own perverted form of sexual politics, luring her into a relationship that he cannot, or will not, bring to completion through sexual intimacy. Unlike a genuine priest, however, the therapist is unable to exercise moral authority in a situation that seems to demand it. She is, for reasons known only to her, fascinated by Tony. She may even be attracted to him. But she can't let any of this surface, even when she is talking to her own therapist.

Not surprisingly, Dr. Melfi is no different from others in Tony Soprano's life. She is tainted by her association with him, by her implicit acceptance of his world as something worthy of rational treatment. On the surface, she doesn't want to know the truth about him, doesn't want to put herself into legal or professional jeopardy by hearing things she might be compelled to report. As a result, the relationship is hideously skewed from the beginning, and it can't go anywhere productive, although Tony can be "helped" to a degree. Helping him is, in itself, an act of complicity in his world.

One watches as Dr. Melfi gets into progressively deeper trouble, taking on many of the traits associated with the Sopranos. Indeed, one of the subtlest moments in the series occurs toward the end of the second season when Dr. Melfi actually imitates (without knowing it) the patented gestures of dismissal associated with Tony's mother. Livia's famous scowl and hand gesture of contempt (which with her is often followed by an ironic "Oh, go away!") is unwittingly reproduced by Dr. Melfi—making her into a type of narcissistic mother herself. (I'm assuming that this was done consciously by the actress or signaled by the writers; or perhaps it was the artist in Lorraine Bracco who knew just what to do. Not all subtlety in art is consciously produced.)

One sees Dr. Melfi slowly unraveling: in restaurants, in her home, with her own therapist. She begins to drink heavily, and her personal life goes to hell. Even her looks seem to degenerate. She apparently finds the world of the Sopranos as addictive as do television viewers. It is difficult to resist a compelling narrative, with its implied (and often realized) violence, and perhaps that is what drove her to become a therapist in the first place. That Tony destroys everyone and everything around him, wittingly or unwittingly, is a point played out in the patient-therapist sessions with astounding ease.

The violence that increasingly dominates the series is, like so much in *The Sopranos,* ambiguously presented. It is both a satire on violence and a presentation of that violence. Inevitably, the series calls on our memory of the *Godfather* films, where violence is used so effectively to keep the audience in a state of almost perpetual suspense. With Tony Soprano and his friends, there is always the possibility of explosion. Christopher, as it were, represents naked aggression, having a thin grip on reality. His attempts to normalize himself, as a scriptwriter or stockbroker, are comical. Again, the casting is adept: Michael Imperioli seems to have been born for this part, the young wise guy. He delivers his dialogue with savvy and perfect timing. And he seems coiled at all times, ready to spring forth in violence, unpredictably.

But Tony himself establishes the model, sets the tone. He has a short fuse, and seems barely able to contain his emotions; he has, indeed, never learned to delay gratification, and he will lash out at those who oppose him. Of course he does so, at times, with considerable anguish, as when he must "whack" his close friend, Pussy, who has betrayed him to the Feds. (I found the last episode of the second season, where Tony takes Pussy for his final ride on the yacht, almost too painful to watch. It is exquisite drama, made all the more dramatic toward the end of the scene when Pussy realizes that, of course, he must be sacrificed. He has been part of the Mob too long to believe they could do otherwise. A wise guy who betrays his own clan must be given a set of concrete shoes.)

That Tony is also a "regular" guy, a family man, is all part of the joke. He can take out the garbage and kill the garbage man on the same errand, sliding from one role to another with apparent ease (although we know the price he pays: anxiety attacks—a secular form of conscience). That Tony has a small army of operatives who will do his violent bidding only amplifies possibilities: if he loses his temper, a lot of heads can roll.

Of course part of what makes Tony so engaging is that he doesn't act simply out of temper; he—unlike many others in his "family"—has a set of guidelines, a code, which governs his behavior. The Mob has its own rules, and Tony is quite capable of reining himself in to act in accordance with these unwritten but perfectly understood rules.

The series also explores the line between "acting" like a gangster and "acting" itself in quite ingenious ways, as when Christopher Moltisanti receives the unlikely gift of a class in theatrical writing from his girlfriend. These scenes are some of the funniest, and shrewdest, in the series. In one episode, the teacher places Christopher before the class, instructing him to act out a scene without words. He is meant to mutter and gesture. But he finds himself quickly transforming before our eyes into a monster of aggression. The class and the audience watching on are both stunned by this transformation, which is altogether typical of the Soprano family. The metafictional element is not lost on the writers of the series, I dare say. They seem to enjoy toying with the play-within-the-play scenario, and the whole thread about Christopher and his Mafia screenplay is an adroit comment on the life-imitating-art trope, amplified by the various allusions to *The Godfather,* the Rosetta Stone of Mafia folklore.

Everyone caught in the aura of Tony Soprano is eventually transformed into something unpleasant, a refraction of Tony's own narcissistic ego. It comes as no surprise, for example, when Carmela increasingly resorts to threats to get her own way in any number of domestic situations. Over the course of three seasons, she becomes gradually more cruel, more calculating, and more willing to accept the laws of the Mob as her own. She has been transformed from the Victorian "angel of the hearth" to a version of Lady Macbeth, in part because she cannot live without the perquisites of middle-class suburban life. She wants what she wants, and Tony has shown her how to get what she wants. He has modeled a way of taking what she thinks is rightfully hers.

One is led to believe that, at first, Carmela was less aware of the "real" nature of her husband's work. This can only be partially true. She doubtless knew exactly what she was getting into when she married Tony. The children, of course, are another story. Meadow in particular seems only gradually to accept her father's work in an explicit way. As she does, however, she becomes more thuggish herself. Her brother, on the other hand, seems to have understood the nature of his circumstances from the outset.

In subtle ways, *The Sopranos* interrogates the American split between home and work. In the television sitcoms of the fifties, it was commonplace to see the father come home from work to the suburban house, where he would find himself having to get involved in the wife's domestic problems and the usual conflicts that preoccupy his children. Often his work intruded, and there was ample room for comedy here. This situation mirrored, as it were, the domestic circumstances of the standard American middle-class family, who saw their lives played out before their eyes in highly idealized forms in *Leave It to Beaver* or *I Love Lucy,* to name only the most obvious sitcoms. *The Sopranos* seems to toy with, to question, to satirize those series and the assumptions about family dynamics that they establish. The most obvious of these is the convention that the family will have no explicit involvement with the father's work; when the father's work intrudes, there is always trouble. Lucy is not supposed to get involved with the famous stars that her husband happens to work with at the club, but she does, and the results are often comic. Darrin in *Bewitched* is not supposed to bring his boss home; but when the boss drops by, there is always mayhem. Work and play are meant to be separate realms, hermetically sealed off from each other.

Things have doubtless changed since the fifties, but there is still an un-spoken rule about the separation of work and family life in the American middle class. It remains one of the splits built into the social system, meant to "protect" the family from the brutality of business. But when the business that supports the family is violence itself, the intrusions and confusions that result are both comic and tragic at the same time; the conflicts that result point up the absurdities of the split.

When Meadow, for example, is taken for a college visit to Colby by her father, it goes without saying that he should shed his role as Mafia don. But the "business" intrudes, and while Meadow is having her interview at the admissions office, Tony sets off after a former associate whom he hap-pens by chance to see. While Meadow is going through the usual ritual in-terview, Tony—instead of twiddling his thumbs in the waiting room, like most middle-class parents—runs off to murder the former associate. That Meadow should notice the blood on him when he picks her up quite won-derfully shows that he has not managed to contain these worlds; they can never really be contained in any case: this was always a lie.

In general, *The Sopranos* holds up a mirror to American middle-class life, and the distortions viewed in that mirror seem exaggerated for the sake of narrative effect. But these effects are not nearly as distorted as we like to imagine. Though comprising less than twenty-five percent of the global vil-lage, we consume over seventy percent of the world's resources. Our gaudy lifestyle, with its insatiable thirst for resources, presupposes a level of vio-lence: against nature, against our world neighbors, against each other. In *The Sopranos,* this violence is normalized, made to appear casual, unremarkable. Even the most extreme instances of violence in the series are played a little tongue-in-cheek.

We can temporarily dismiss violent acts by the Soprano clan as just an-other example of Mafia shenanigans, and as viewers of the series we may wish to reassure ourselves by saying, "There they go again, those Mafiosi." They are not Us. But I have found myself circling back in memory to those mo-ments of violence, horrified as I become more aware of the violence that is now normalized in American life. I realize how I have been suppressing in myself the memory of state violence (and coercion), historical violence, and my own aggressive urges, and how this repression is part and parcel of being a male in America at the dawn of the twenty-first century.

FRESH GARBAGE

THE GANGSTER AS
SUBURBAN TRICKSTER

Fred Gardaphé

Look beneath your lid some morning . . .
The world's a can for your fresh garbage.

                    —*Jay Ferguson, "Fresh Garbage"*

If you seek the monuments of the bourgeoisie, go to the suburbs
and look around.

                    —*Robert Fishman,* Bourgeois Utopia

INTRODUCTION

There was a guy in our old neighborhood we used to call "The Ragsaline Man." He got his nickname because he kept calling out "Ragsaline, ragsaline," as he drove an ancient truck slowly through the neighborhood looking for rags and old iron and other junk. With grandparents who were

Italian immigrants, I was not surprised that this man could treasure other people's garbage; we were all taught that it was a sin to waste, and to avoid that sin we had to develop new ways of seeing.

In our house you were called on anything that might potentially be wasted. We ate parts of animals that butchers used to throw away. You didn't leave food on your plate, as I later learned most "mericans" did to be polite and to show that they were not "pigs." Anything not eaten in one of our family meals would find its way into subsequent meals. Clothes that no longer fit were passed on to those who could wear them or they were shipped to Italy; the clothes that were no longer wearable would be torn neatly into rags for cleaning. Nothing was wasted. Sabato Rodia, an Italian immigrant, provides a good example of how a work of art could be created of junk: seashells, shards of glass, and ceramic tile. His "Watts Towers," located in south Los Angeles, is called, by Nick Costanza Shay, the protagonist of Don DeLillo's novel *Underworld,* "a kind of swirling free-souled noise, a jazz cathedral" where Nick finds that his "own ghost father was living in the walls."[1] This tradition, of seeing garbage in a fresh light, of not wasting anything, of making something out of nothing, of seeing one's ancestors in the result, is one that will help us better understand David Chase's *The Sopranos.*

There can be no doubt that Chase, the creator and executive producer of this hit television series, conceived the program in the tradition and spirit of the U.S. gangster film and executed it as a commentary on not only the genre but contemporary life in the United States. As a crafty "ragpicker," he cast an eye over the garbage heap of film characters, picked up the discarded gangster, dusted him off, and gave him new life by setting him down in the suburbs, where today over sixty percent of Americans live. In doing so, he has breathed new life into this cultural icon that has captured the attention of American audiences since his first appearance in the early silent films. But Chase has given us fresh garbage.

In the novel *Underworld,* Don DeLillo presents a garbage archeologist who gives the keynote address at a waste management industry convention. The novel's protagonist, an Italian American, explains the professor's theory that civilization is the result of garbage: "We had to find ways to discard our waste, to use what we couldn't discard, to reprocess what we couldn't use. Garbage pushed back. It mounted and spread. And it forced us to develop the logic and rigor that would lead to systematic investigations of reality, to science, art, music, mathematics."[2] DeLillo concocts an interesting notion, especially if we apply it to the development of American bourgeois culture.

Thorstein Veblin's classic, *Theory of the Leisure Class,* taught us all how to make sense of the consumer culture of capitalism, and his notions of "conspicuous consumption" and "conspicuous waste" can help us overcome the simplification of knee-jerk responses to *The Sopranos. The Sopranos* matters most because it reflects U.S. capitalism at its height. "In order to be reputable it must be wasteful," writes Veblen. And *The Sopranos* fulfills this mandate better than any other television program. It is creative as it is critical. It is historical as it is hysterical. Tony Soprano, a partner in a waste management company (among other legal and illegal businesses) is not only a purveyor of garbage, but a dramatic embodiment of the waste produced by postmodern U.S. consumer culture.

Only if we see Tony Soprano as a trickster figure can we begin to explain America's fascination with gangsters and the success of the HBO series. What we have then is the need for a society to have a figure that can represent fringe behavior against which the center of society can formulate its values and identity. The Mafia myth has thus served an important function in American society in both defining what is American and what is acceptable behavior in American society.

What makes *The Sopranos* worth watching and worth talking about is the way that Chase uses Tony Soprano's actions to speak to contemporary life in the United States. As Wallace Katz writes: "Even though Tony Soprano is a criminal, he is a mirror image of ourselves. Which is why his existence opens up a window on the dilemmas of American society at the dawn of the twenty-first century."[3] Katz sees Tony Soprano as "a kind of contemporary Babbit, who embodies the culture wars—between virtue and happiness, between disciplined 'character' and the protean self, between dying traditions and a vacuous modernity—that currently tear apart the American soul and keep us from creating the new moral perspective, cultural identity, and, above all, new politics that we need.[4]

Tony Soprano's movement from urban ethnic to assimilated suburban American is mirrored in the signature opening montage that Katz says "tells a story about generational change and social mobility, the American Dream."[5] A close look at the images that make up this montage helps us understand how this happens. The sequence begins with a shot of the ceiling of the Lincoln

Tunnel that connects Manhattan to New Jersey. We are in a vehicle driving west, away from the city. Most of the images are presented through the driver's point of view; all we see of the driver are his eyes in the rear-view mirror. The car clock reads 10:22 A.M., so either Tony Soprano is coming home from an all-nighter in the city, or from an early morning meeting. In any case, he is returning home. We see a plane coming in, he lights a cigar, he's on the turnpike, bypassing the city of Newark. This is followed by a series of images of working-class sites: oil tanks, factories, a blue-collar neighborhood, the church, cemetery, Satriale's Pork Store, Pizzaland. Soon the working-class neighborhoods give way to wider, tree-lined streets that lead into upper-middle-class estates. The sequence ends with the car stopping at the top of the driveway of the Soprano home. We have just completed a journey from the old city to the new suburb, through tunnels forged by people like Tony Soprano's ancestors, through a working-class neighborhood where Tony might have been born, ending up in the gangster's plush upper-middle-class suburban estate near the peak of U.S. social class. This is the stereotypical journey taken by those who chase the American dream.

These opening images are accompanied by the series theme song, "Woke Up This Morning" by the group A3, which sets up a commentary on the internal life of the protagonist. The song recounts a philosophical bout with mortality that happens when a middle-aged man returns home after a three-day drinking binge and plays music that reminds him of the blues and jazz greats such as Charles Mingus, Eric Dolphy, Billie Holiday, Ella Fitzgerald, Muddy Waters, and Howlin' Wolf. The philosophical rant contains the following lyrics: "You woke up this morning, got yourself a gun,/ Mama always said you'd be the Chosen One."

As the oldest, and only son, in an Italian American family, Tony is the one chosen to take over his father's way of life, a life that requires the use of violence in order to sustain itself. But his father never explained that life to Tony: "Your Papa never told you about right and wrong," the song continues. In fact, Tony is a rarity among Italian Americans. Most sons of gangsters never did follow in their father's footsteps as each generation, through money and education, found more socially acceptable ways of achieving the trappings of middle- and upper-class American life. The next verse, about what happened when "the Blues walked into town," speaks to the central dilemma that our protagonist is facing—depression. Tony only begins to deal with his depression after he suffers physically from stress symptoms. On the road to finding a cure, Tony begins the task of confronting the effects of his gangster life.

Chase's success with this series, as we will see, depends not on his ability to represent Italian American culture—something that has irked quite a few Americans of Italian descent, some of whom have tried to stop the projection if not the production of the program—but on his ability to make us see the garbage produced by contemporary American life. Through Tony Soprano, the Italian American has become American. By examining the way Chase uses Tony Soprano's Italianness, we can gain great insight into the alienation caused by U.S. capitalist culture of the twenty-first century. This chapter examines Chase's reconstruction of the gangster figure and its migration into postmodern U.S. suburban culture. I begin with a survey of the larger tradition of the gangster figure in U.S. entertainment so that we get a sense of where Tony Soprano ranks in terms of his fictional ancestors. This is followed by an examination of what the show is telling us about middle-class life in the postmodern United States of America.

THE GANGSTER IN AMERICAN CULTURE

Hardly an episode of *The Sopranos* passes without some nod to or comment upon an earlier classic depiction of the gangster. In the opening episode, we see cutaways to Al Capone and head shots of famous actors playing gangsters (Humphrey Bogart, Dean Martin, and Edward G. Robinson) as Christopher Moltisanti (played by Michael Imperioli) shoots a rival in the garbage business. The music in the background is Muddy Waters's "I'm a Man." The gangster that young Christopher aspires to be and believes he has become through this murder has typically embodied the traits that the dominant culture represses in reality, yet adores as entertainment. The gangster has become a marker of ethnicity and a mode of being a man in contemporary American life. The gangster has also become a model for moving from poverty or working class to middle or even upper class, a trope for signifying the gain of cultural power that comes through class mobility.

I want to emphasize that I am speaking of the gangster as an artistic device rather than as an actual thug who belongs to a group of organized criminals. The gangster I am most interested in is the one created by an artist to speak for some philosophical dilemma faced in the time of the author's life.

This gangster is usually the one around whom others form a feudal fraternity. Within this old-fashioned system, the gangster/leader receives the proceeds of everyone's work; it is he who then doles out shares that he deems appropriate for each member. In return, the gangster provides direction, protection, and a calming sense of order. The gangster is the man with the plan, the man of action who knows how to get things done and who has a strong sense of two worlds: the one inside and the other outside the gang, and he bridges the two like no other can. The gangster, then, in the hands of American artists, becomes a telling figure in the tale of American class, race, gender, and ethnicity; and in the hands of American artists of Italian descent, the gangster becomes a figure that reflects the autobiography of an immigrant group just as it reflects the fantasy of a native population.

As a way of structuring our understanding of David Chase's version of the American gangster, I divide the use of the gangster figure into three stages. The first is gangster portrayal as minstrelsy. Like the blackface minstrelsy of the nineteenth century, the early use of the gangster figure was a means of exploiting and controlling a variant culture through performance. In this way, the majority culture could co-opt and control the subculture while defusing any threat posed by the difference the Italian immigrant brought to American culture. This stage begins in the earliest films, and takes off with the rise of Al Capone, through the earliest talkies, and fades during the Vietnam War period. Here I would include films such as *Little Caesar* (1930) and *Scarface* (1931). A second stage takes place when Italian Americans begin to use the figure of the gangster to historicize the Italian experience in the United States. Films that reflect this stage of historical reconstruction include *The Godfather* (1972) and *Goodfellas* (1990). The third stage takes place when Italian Americans begin to parody and renounce the figure as a means of gaining control of their own stories. Dramatic productions that represent this stage include *The Sopranos* (1998-present) and Richard Vetere's play *Gangster Apparel* (2001). Each of these stages represents a variation of the American gangster myth from its rise to its fall.

Recent work on blackface minstrelsy can be applied to the study of the gangster to help us understand the rise of the gangster figure in U.S. entertainment, for it is not long after the end of blackface minstrel shows that we see the Italian replace the black as the subject of imitation in popular culture. Eric Lott, in *Love and Theft*, tells us that "The black mask offered a way to play with collective fears of a degraded and threatening—and male—Other while at the same time maintaining some symbolic control over them."[6] This is precisely the same thing that happens to Italians in the gangster films of the 1930s. Another dimension that the gangster figure shares with the black-faced figure is overt sexuality. Lott writes: "Bold swagger, irrepressible desire, sheer bodily display: in a real sense the minstrel man *was* the penis, that organ returning in a variety of contexts, at times ludicrous, at others rather less so." As we will see, the Italian male gangster fulfills a similar role. Again, Lott provides a key perspective: "What appears to have been appropriated were certain kinds of masculinity. To put on the cultural forms of 'blackness' was to engage in a complex affair of manly mimicry."[7] The gangster figure was presented as a way of being a man. These representations, enacted by Jewish actors such as Edward G. Robinson and Paul Muni, also convey a sense of projected fantasy. As Nathan Huggins in *Harlem Renaissance* noted, "minstrel characters were simply trash-bin projections of white fantasy, vague fleshy signifiers that allowed whites to indulge at a distance all that they found repulsive and fearsome."[8] This minstrelsy stage as it applies to Italian Americans is noted by its distortion, if not disfigurement, of Italian culture, ostensibly for plot purposes, but actually as a means of maintaining power over the foreign elements that were attracting attentions and desires. One of the great distortions in this early gangster minstrelsy is the repression of the role of women in Italian culture and the replacement of the mother/son paradigm with the father/son paradigm. As we will see, this aspect of this first stage is picked up in the second stage by Italian American artists. This first stage also distorts the communal aspect of Italian culture, replacing it with the American stress on individuality. The Italian gangster, as he is depicted in this stage, rises out of poverty or from America's working class through a world that demands not his individuality, but his ability to contribute to the betterment of the entire community of criminals. The fame he achieves in American society and the rise of his individuality separates him from his group and soon leads to his demise.

The gangster as we know him today is a strange mix of fact and fiction. More than an urban evolution of the western outlaw, the gangster came into American culture at a time when great change was occurring in American society. Al Capone's rise to gangster god status came during America's "Roaring Twenties," a time of great excess and changing morality caused by a booming economy. In response to this mixture, reactionary religious forces joined other conservative elements of U.S. society to lobby for the prohibition of the production and sale of alcohol. This repression created a ripe opportunity for smart street thugs to thrive. A legend in his own time, Capone became a symbol of contemporary power and that legend became the basis for the many gangster films that emerged in the 1930s. Cover boy of the March 1930 *Time* magazine, Capone became the subject of some of the most popular films of this period: *Little Caesar* (1931); *Scarface: Shame of a Nation* (1932), and *Public Enemy* (1931). The gangster figure emerged in U.S. popular culture at a time when the nation was shifting from an agrarian to an industrial-based economy; this was also a time when immigration to the United States was at its highest and xenophobia was rampant.

David Ruth, in *Inventing the Public Enemy: The Gangster in American Culture, 1918–1934,* argues that as America's urban centers grew, as the U.S. economy was becoming more corporatized, and as the government became more bureaucratized, the American was losing a traditional sense of individuality. Amid this social upheaval, the gangster became "a central cultural figure because he helped Americans master this changing social world."[9] Prior to the invention of the gangster, Ruth tells us, crime was presented through a deranged individual who performed his deeds single-handedly in dark and dreary urban ghettos. Based on the realities of the 1920s and 1930s, crime scenes in early gangster films moved from "ethnic" ghettos to downtown commercial centers. This enabled the criminal to resemble more closely those in the rising business class, and less so those dark, ethnic foreigners of earlier depictions. Thus the criminal was rising in class and assimilating to mainstream culture at the same time American urban white ethnics were trying to do the same. Easier access to stylish consumption, through fancy dress and cars, blurred the earlier lines that separated social class. As street criminals began associating with the upper echelons of society, it became harder to tell the gangster from the corporate elite.

The prototype for this gangster, says Ruth, is Al Capone, an "attractive and repulsive" figure that "illuminated the lives of urban Americans." The transference of fact into fiction returns in the next generation as fiction alters fact. New York police detective Remo Franceschini observed during his surveillance of John Gotti that real gangsters had started imitating the characters in *The Godfather* films. After a generation one could hardly tell the difference between the real and artificial gangster.

Capone's story, as a microcosm of how the individual could move from poverty to wealth, from ignominy to fame, also epitomized the gangster's adoption of corporate strategies to run illegal businesses. *Little Caesar*, based on Capone's life, catapulted the gangster into American consciousness, and led the way for the creation of a new type of film. The great social impact of the film has been attributed to its being one of the earliest talkies, but the film did more than help us listen to the gangster's voice and hear his violence. *Scarface*, written by Chicago reporter Ben Hecht, directed by Howard Hawks, and produced by Howard Hughes, faced intense pressure from religious and civic leaders. In production during the same time as *Little Caesar, Scarface* was held back by the Hays' Production Code censors, who insisted on the inclusion of a scene that Hawks refused to create. Eventually Hughes approved the addition of a scene in which a newspaper editor leads a group of civic leaders, including one Italian American, in a discussion of the need to eliminate gangsters.

After these films, the gangster film was never quite the same. Pressure from inside the industry, through Will Hays and the Motion Pictures Producers and Distributors Association, helped the industry shift its focus from the gangsters to the good guys who chased them. Films that featured the gangster were relegated to B-movie status as the former stars of gangster films began taking on the roles of the G-men and police. The gangster in American film would remain in the shadows of Hollywood lights until Francis Ford Coppola took on Mario Puzo's *The Godfather*. It wasn't until after *The Godfather* films had rekindled an interest and renewed the obsession with the gangster figure that *Scarface* (1931) was returned to circulation.

The censors could not eliminate the desire of non-gangsters to peek into that forbidden world from time to time. Film scholar Jonathan Munby tells us, "The gangster film is a genre like pornography and the horror film, held in contempt socially and intellectually not because it may corrupt and not because it is artistically inferior to other kinds of film but because it realizes our dreams, exposes our deepest psychic urges. . . . The genre speaks to not merely our fascination/repulsion with aspects of our socioeconomic milieu that we prefer to shut our eyes to but also to our fascination/repulsion with the most haunting depths of ourselves."[10] Munby sees the gangster as providing us with a view into our world from a different perspective: "If there is a problem the society is worried about or a fantasy it is ready to support, odds are it can be located in the gangster."[11]

As Jack Shadoian points out in his study of gangster films, entitled *Dreams and Dead Ends,* the gangster film can make us "see things that would otherwise be hard to see. It locates an underworld, a world beneath the surface and shows it to us—a literal embodiment of those things that exist but are difficult to see in American life."[12] Shadoian finds the gangster embodying "Two fundamental and opposing American ideologies—a contradiction in thought between America as a land of opportunity and the vision of a classless, democratic society."[13] The gangster functions as the scapegoat for the obsessive desire for self-advancement, and unrelieved class conflicts are played out in films. He becomes, for the United States, the only sanctioned soldier in the class war; and ultimately he teaches us that it is a losing battle. The gangster is also a guide to the underworld, taking us places that we might never go on our own. Other themes surrounding the gangster include the disintegration and destruction of the family; the substitution of a "false family"—the gang—for the real family; and a son in a New World rebelling against a father from an Old World.

The truth is that the fiction of the gangster is stronger than the facts, and the facts of American history will never be as attractive as the myths that have been created around the gangster. Prior to Puzo's *The Godfather,* the gangster was usually a singular individual whose gang dissolved when he was jailed, killed, or reformed. Don Corleone is the first fictional gangster who is not a psychopath. Through filmmakers Francis Ford Coppola, Martin Scorsese, and Brian De Palma, and writers Mario Puzo, Gay Talese, Frank Lentricchia, Don DeLillo, and Anthony Valerio, most of us have come to know the American gangster as a more rounded figure, a man who thinks before he acts, one who rarely pulls the trigger of a gun. From Mario Puzo's *The Godfather* to *Lucchesi and The Whale,* the latest novel by Frank Lentricchia, Italian American culture has taken hold of the figure of the gangster and elevated it from a common criminal to a god of sorts that can help us understand much about ourselves and our societies.

The second stage of the gangster begins, I believe, with Mario Puzo's novel *The Godfather,* and the films based on it. At this stage, we see the Italian American artist using an accepted and profitable public vehicle to tell a personal story. The mother/son paradigm employed by Puzo in his *The Fortunate Pilgrim* is exchanged for the father/son in *The Godfather.* We see this repeated in most of the films that are derived out of the Puzo/Coppola work and in the work of Martin Scorsese. In one of the last interviews of his life, Puzo admitted that he had modeled Don Corleone after his mother. In this way he contributed to the humanization of the gangster and the connection of the gangster to the larger forces of American culture.

By connecting the story of the development of American capitalism to the immigration saga of Italian Americans, gangster films from *Scarface* to *The Godfather* and beyond have fashioned a convenient symbol toward which revolutionary rage can be deflected. They have also, inadvertently perhaps, set up the model for media representations of gangsters as real human beings, as capable of showing affection to a kitten as they are of killing relatives who are perceived as having put the family in danger. The original Don Corleone (Vito) enables the family to rise from poverty to riches, as the heir, Michael, refines his father's tricks of the trade to help the family thrive in a post-immigration world in which the trickster gains acceptance as an American businessman, but loses his family.

The third stage, the one in which the gangster figure is renounced, begins with the television series *The Sopranos*. Now that Home Box Office has sold this series to markets throughout the world, the American gangster may once again be a prime model for imitation and again be the primary association many make with the United States of America. This show has generated a great deal of national discussion and little of it goes beyond arguing for or against it. *The Sopranos* has become to the United States of the new millennium what *Dallas* was to the 1980s, and in this respect it reveals that the Italians have finally, after more than 100 years of living in this country, assimilated sufficiently enough to warrant a prime-time cable show about life in suburbia. But people are missing the mark when they try to limit interpretation of these characters to their superficial Italian American identities. This hit series signals a major change in what the gangster represents and in what is happening to the American way of life.

The original American gangsters represented a traditional, patriarchal sense of manhood that came from an old European model. The key to portraying this sense of manhood was that violence could be used to bring and sustain honor, a notion that is being clung to all the tighter in a dying patriarchal mode of organizing our world. And for this type of gangster, the swarthy European-looking Italians made for instant identity with the type; after all, America has always compared itself to Europe to determine its difference.

The Sopranos, if it has anything to teach us, is about the (r)emasculation of the traditional American male, historically presented to us through films such as those starring John Wayne. The American man is changing; this is what *The Sopranos* is telling us. There is only one way I know by which a man can be made into a soprano; metaphorically this is what is happening to Tony Soprano, who happens to be a gangster in a time in which traditional notions of manhood are reeling from the challenges of feminism and gay liberation.

Like many male baby boomers in the throes of middle age, Tony is trying to figure out who he is and why he does what he does. He has come to realize that he is not the man his father was and that his own son will not be able to carry on the family business. Trapped between the past and the present with an unimaginable future, he begins to feel weak and after a couple of incidents in which he loses consciousness, he visits a doctor. When his doctor suggests he see a psychiatrist to help him deal with his stress, he stumbles upon a way of feeling better; but for Tony Soprano, it comes with a cost, and that cost is betraying the tribal code of keeping silent, especially to strangers. Tony Soprano begins to lose a traditional Italian sense of manhood by first talking about his work, and second by talking about it with a woman. Hesitant at first, he finds that as he continues to talk, he begins to question the traditional order of things and this leads him to question his role as a husband, a father, a son, and a gangster.

To Tony, the history of organized crime has become a poetry, an art, the history of which comforts him as it gives him a sense of being connected to a past. He has turned the actions of past gangsters into myths, as though his father belonged to some type of golden age of gangsterhood. He becomes philosophic as he contemplates these myths, and the more he thinks about them, the more he can see that they are nothing but fragile constructions that shatter easily. The values of the immigrant generation are lost, transformed, from using waste to making waste. Ultimately we, if not Tony, learn that he has never matured. In an early episode he exclaims to his daughter that "In this house it's still 1954." Ultimately, Tony's immaturity has kept him from adapting to a changing world in which women and even children might speak frankly about sex at the dinner table. Tony Soprano believes he is constantly being besieged by forces bent on making him conform to various expectations: the FBI, his neighbors, his mistress, his children, his wife.

Without a solid sense of self, he constantly wavers from the attacks on his ego. As he begins to explore just who he is, he opens up the possibility that being a gangster might not be such a good choice after all.

Certainly, after Tony Soprano there can be no Mafia, in the traditional sense, in the Italian way. When Tony breaks "omerta," he is no longer behaving the way a man should, as the Spanish source "ombredad" suggests. This behavior, coded and displayed by the Spaniard aristocracy who occupied Italy, says a man should be known through actions more than words: "Le parole sono femmine; I fatti sono maschi," goes an Italian saying. Words are feminine; actions are masculine.

One reason *The Sopranos* is so popular is that, on a superficial level, it gives its audience an acceptable bad guy whose job it is to uphold an alternative system that lives off capitalism without contributing its "fair share" of dues to the power brokers; he comes from a tribe that decided it wouldn't work hard to make someone else rich. Unlike the operatic qualities of Coppola's films, *The Sopranos* features typical American family qualities radiated by the program's form and content. The Soprano family functions in the everyday world of middle-class America, but maintains an Old World sense of structure and obligation that separates it from the neighbors. And while the patriarchal mode of that world is weakening, its matriarchal foundation is surfacing. Whether it's through Tony's wife, his mother, or his psychiatrist, the power of women to change the world is featured as never before. Whereas Coppola gives us the feminine power of Connie Corleone, who essentially mimics the violent ways of her brothers, David Chase presents the strong women of the Soprano family, who wield power and who shape reality through their hearts and minds. There is a trajectory started in the early episodes of the series that suggests a development of this gangster that we haven't seen in any of the earlier representations. And after thirty-nine hours of depiction over three seasons, this trajectory has continued to maintain its hold on its audience. This suggests that the Italian American has created a gangster that can speak beyond the confines of an ethnic ghetto, about issues that concern not just cops and robbers. Of all the issues we can connect to the show, the one that I believe holds the most promise psychologically is the return of the Italian paradigm of the mother/son relationship to the male psyche.

This mother/son paradigm is one that fosters community instead of individuality. The dominant story in U.S. literature and film is one that stresses self-invention, often through a son rebelling against his father, possibly becoming reunited with the father as a prodigal son. The dominant paradigm in Italy has almost always stressed self-connection to society through the son who protects his mother and the rest of the family. Gaetano Cipolla, an authority on Italian culture, writes:

> The mother's role, shaped by thousands of years of history, continues to our day almost unchanged. She nurtures physically and psychologically, she performs social duties in observance of time-worn formulas, she sacrifices her whole life to her family, denying herself in the process and becoming a victim of her dedication to others. Her devotion to her family is so complete that as a Sicilian proverb has it *"La matri senti li guai di lu mutu"* (The Mother feels the troubles of the mute.) Inevitably, however, in the battle between the children's desire for freedom and the mother's desire to maintain the status quo—for this reason Leonardo Sciascia considered Sicilian mothers a cause of the stagnation in Sicilian society—conflicts emerge and mothers begin to consider themselves victims, adopting what may be called a martyr's syndrome. . . . Angelo Costanzo suggested that Sicilian women everywhere eventually end up conforming with the image of the *matri addulurata,* that is, the sorrowful mother who grieves for the loss of her son. It is not a coincidence that in Sicily, out of all the possible scenes of the madonna's life, the most pervasive is certainly that of the grieving mother.[14]

While Tony Soprano is not Sicilian, he is of southern Italian culture, and heir to this matri-focal culture. As we will see, *The Sopranos* has its origins not in the U.S. feminist movement, but in the development of suburban culture in the United States that resurrects the power that women have always held in Italian culture.

THE TRICKSTER IN THE SUBURB

A look around the suburbs today will tell you that they are no longer the utopic havens that once promised wealthy urbanites refuge from the ills of city life. Some suburbs—literally built atop landfills of the waste of cities bursting beyond their original boundaries—are quickly succumbing to the same overcrowding and pollution that led to their creation. The suburbs as

we have come to know them appear to have been simply a phase, what
Robert Fishman calls "the point of transition between two decentralized eras:
the preindustrial rural era and the postindustrial information society." Fishman calls the new developments "technoburbs" that have "renewed the link-
age of work and residence"[15] that once characterized the earliest city life, the
very life that the suburbs had tried to separate in their attempt to provide a
better relationship between man and nature. There is no better vantage point
from which to view life in these new technoburbs than in *The Sopranos*.

This representation of suburban life recalls earlier television shows
that portrayed suburban family life, such as *Leave It to Beaver* and *Father
Knows Best*. Only now the father's job is that of a boss in New Jersey organized crime. The earliest suburbs, going back to Chaucer's time, were
where "robbers and thieves instinctively huddle secretly and fearfully together."[16] But suburbia not only restructured man's relationship to his
work and his family, it also expressed "a complex and compelling vision of
the modern family freed from the corruption of the city, restored to har-
mony with nature, endowed with wealth and independence yet protected
by a close-knit, stable community."[17] All this begins to change when
gangsters find their way in.

As we eventually learn through flashbacks, Tony Soprano is the only son
of Johnny and Livia Soprano. He is raised with two sisters, one older and one
younger, in Newark's Little Italy. At some point after the death of his father,
he and his family, which includes his wife Carmela and their children
Meadow and Anthony, Jr., take up residence at the symbolically loaded address 633 Stag Trail Road, North Caldwell, New Jersey, 07006, in Essex
County, one of the wealthiest counties in the United States.

The Sopranos' movement from the city to the suburbs mirrors the migration of ethnic groups who, after spending a generation or two in the
city, move away, searching for their promised land. But as they move away
from their old neighborhoods, they also leave behind their old ways of
being. City life requires identity with your neighborhood and your culture. Life in the suburbs requires assimilation, which demands that one
lose the trappings of the original culture, including one's original language. While Tony Soprano learns to think of himself as a white, assimilated American, he also sees himself as different from those whites he calls
"mayonnaise," like his neighbor Dr. Bruce Cusamano, Tony's personal

physician. Assimilation requires a separation of the generations, and this is something that we begin to see happening in the Soprano family.

In all the episodes of the series, there is only the briefest of references to the immigrant generation. One of these occurs when Tony walks his daughter into a church and tells her that his grandfather helped to build the church, not as an architect, but as a bricklayer. He takes much pride in the fact that his grandfather contributed to one of society's fundamental structures, but it is a structure that he has long ago stopped worshiping in. The next generation is represented through Tony's mother Livia and his Uncle Corrado, or Junior. Tony comes to understand that it is easy to realize history; the danger comes in making it. The history of immigration was filled with people who made incredible sacrifices, and while Tony has come to know the past, he can't possibly foresee what his future will be. Like the people in the famous Marshall McLuhan metaphor, Tony is driving forward while looking in his rearview mirror. He and his wife represent a third generation and his children, Meadow and Anthony, Jr., the fourth.

As a card-carrying member of suburban life, Tony surrounds himself and his family with all the appropriate accessories that enable him to conspicuously consume. He drives a Suburban and not the Cadillac of the earlier generation of American gangsters, and his wife has a Mercedes Benz. His children attend Verbum Dei, a private secondary school; he has a pool in his backyard and gym equipment in his basement. The suburban home, surrounded by greenery, enables privacy and invisibility from neighbors. One can only imagine what goes on next door, as when Tony's psychiatrist, Dr. Melfi, dining at the Cusamanos', goes to the bathroom to see if she can catch a glimpse of her patient. She hears a terrifying moaning which she will never know came from Tony benchpressing his weights.

Another middle-class accoutrement is Tony's boat, appropriately named the *Stugots*. If you didn't get the sense that Chase was playing with Italian American culture before then, this ought to do it. No Italian American would name a power boat after his penis. (*Stugots* is dialect for "sto cazzo" or "Questo cazzo," which translates as "this penis.") This powerboat, often referred to as a "penis boat," becomes the site for bonding with his son, for disposing of unwanted problems, and for the regular rendevous with mistresses. The naming of boats becomes significant again in episode thirteen, when Tony kills one of Junior's hit men in a boat appropriately named *Villain II*. Chase creatively uses these trappings to obliquely condemn the actions of his characters.

Tony's entrée into middle class does not come without its downside. In episode ten, Tony presents his doctor with real Cuban cigars, the illegality of which tantalizes Dr. Cusamano and tempts him to offer Tony a golf outing at the country club. Tony joins the doctor and two other businessmen, who are obsessed with Tony's reputation and try to get him to reinforce their stereotypes and myths about the Mafia. These men, who discuss their business ventures in the same secretive tones that Tony and his wise guys plan their crimes, reveal that they are really no better morally than Tony and his henchmen. Outwardly there is no difference between these businessmen and Tony Soprano, but on the inside, Chase makes us identify with the honesty of Tony Soprano and not with the two-faced behavior of the suburbanites. Dr. Cusamano and his buddies represent the traditional, accepted way up the economic ladder and into upper-middle-class suburbia—through education. Tony Soprano has made it into their neighborhood without more than a year and a half of college education. His presence shatters the illusion that the suburbs belong to those who work hard and follow the moral road, and helps us see that it is the accumulation of money that matters. But while Tony has made it to the world of the wealthy, he struggles to remain loyal to what he perceives as his ancestral heritage. Just what this heritage consists of is never defined by Chase, and is so rarely articulated in dramatic productions that one gets the feeling that there's not a director out there who has a good sense of just what Italian American culture is. This is another reason why people should not become obsessed by what they might perceive as negative portrayals of Italian Americans in the series. As a storyteller, Chase uses what every major storyteller has depended upon since the beginning of time: easily identified types that represent, not realities, but possibilities. It's not Chase's job to represent reality; after all, he's not doing a documentary. Those who cannot see this need to pay closer attention to the many signals he provides to remind us he is telling a story, from the titles of episodes to the continuous dialogue with entertainment history that goes on in each episode. If there is any group of Italian Americans who might have a right to protest representation in the series, it's the tiny number of contemporary Italian American gangsters.

If life in the suburbs conditions Tony Soprano to act like he's not a criminal, it also exposes him to greater female influence than those gangsters who came before him. With the creation of the suburbs, the home becomes the sphere of female power as work and home, formerly integrated in urban life, become separated, with the men's sphere of influence belonging to life out-side the home, and the women's inside the home. If Tony finds it necessary to conduct business in his home, he takes it to his basement and talks in code, a gangster jargon of sorts that keeps his meanings ambiguous. Within the home Carmela gains power and the opportunity to lead the family down a morally correct path. This, as Fishman suggests, was inherent in the cre-ation of the earliest suburbs: "The city was not just crowded, dirty, and un-healthy; it was immoral. Salvation itself depended on separating the woman's sacred world of family and children from the profane metropolis. Yet this separation could not jeopardize a man's constant attendance to his busi-ness. . . . This was the problem, and suburbia was to be the ultimate solu-tion."[18] This idea was advanced early on in American history by Catharine Beecher, author of five influential books dealing with domestication, who wrote that "the 'cult of true womanhood' is linked to the home with piety and purity."[19] This is an important point that is not missed by Chase as he places Tony in a number of situations in which he must come to depend on women. Chase also realizes this when he has Tony move his aging mother out of her home. In the process of relocation, which threatens to destroy her power, his mother turns on him and suggests to her brother-in-law that Tony might be better off dead, which leads to an attempted assassination.

Carmela's power, inside the house, is usually manifested in her kitchen, where she feeds her family and friends, and where she often disciplines and counsels her children. Seduced by the materiality of middle-class life that provides her with safety and comfort, she compromises her morality in order to build a sense of security through the accumulation of wealth. Carmela's power dynamics are often played out at her kitchen table, where she, as the provider of good food, can seduce her guests into giving her sympathy, pro-viding favors, and listening to her instructions. Chase realizes this power dy-namic and has Carmela use food the way her husband uses threats of violence. In one episode, Carmela's power of suggestion, expressed through a ricotta pie, exacts an important letter of recommendation from an influential and reluctant party for her daughter's college application.

However, the Soprano house is often very much unlike the homes of typical Italian Americans. For many years, Italian American culture has been preserved in the homes, and over the years, more likely than not, in the basement, or what Italian Americans have come to call the "basciument," where grandpa made wine, where grandma had a second kitchen, and now where many store material legacies and memories. Outside celebrations such as religious fests became the most important public presentation of Italian American culture, but these annual events were never frequent enough to protect Italian American culture from the regular mass media bombardment of negative stereotypes. Italian American identity, for the most part, has been practiced in the home, where Italian Americans have kept their ethnic trappings in their basements, where their culture is safe inside family celebrations. But Tony and Carmela Soprano's basement is void of such legacies.

CONCLUSION

It was in the 1960s, when slogans like "Power to the People" surfaced to shake up a working-class complacency, that Italian Americans gained their share of power in a society that only a generation earlier had exploited them as workers. The gangster became the symbol of the transformation of the Italian American male from powerless worker to a broker of power. The gangster took power and became an accepted figure for that task. He became a parasite to the legal host of an economic system that had kept him trapped until he took his future into his own hands, along with his gun. This was not a revolutionary, but a reactionary act to which few have paid attention. As Michael Klein observed: "Hollywood films . . . are often fantasies, in some cases fantasies of a special kind in that in restructuring the past, heightening/stylizing the present, or projecting a future, they may defamiliarize and thus clarify aspects of their audience's present situation, or provide a forum for the expression of contradictions, concerns and feelings that the dominant culture represses."[20] In many respects, Chase grasps this concept better than any film artist today. His understanding that you can't make a gangster film like the old ones extends to Tony, who realizes that he cannot be a gangster in the old-fashioned sense of the word, and that in order to survive in this new, postmodern world, he will have to find a language that he can use to, first, communicate with himself, and second, manipulate the world around him.

Tony Soprano is the last of the wise guys and serves as a pivotal figure in the development of wise men. The end of the wise guys and the beginning of wise men then entails developing the skills to gain knowledge and use it instead of violence to solve problems. It is by using knowledge, not physical force, that boys become men, and wise guys become wise men. Indicted for murder, they turn state's evidence and go into the witness protection program, gaining new identities. While this is merely hinted at in *The Sopranos,* it becomes quite evident in Richard Vetere's play *Gangster Apparel.* In a recent revision of a 1995 production, Vetere strengthens his renunciation of the gangster figure and uses him in a sincere attempt to make sense of the influence of Italian culture on American culture.

Vetere understands that Italian American culture is a culture of indirection, and makes the point that to leave Little Italy is to move into the world of irony and to use a language that's not ambiguous. This becomes evident in the exchange toward the end of the play, in a section he added since its 1996 publication. The play's only two characters find themselves in the western United States with new identities provided by the government's witness protection program. Joey tells Louie about how life is different with his new girlfriend.

> JOEY: The words she uses, Louie. Willow Jane wouldn't even think about
>   using that kind of language. She reminds me of my mother that way.
>   Let me tell you something, I am learning out here that out here you are
>   what you say, you are what you think, you are what you do.
> LOUIE: And where is "out here" my friend?
> JOEY: It's America, Louie. The America I never knew was real. When I was
>   growin up, I thought we had only three choices. Be a cop, a priest or a
>   wise guy. Now I know there are other ways to go.[21]

Through this exchange Vetere suggests that renunciation of the gangster figure requires learning things you never knew before. Joey goes on to show Louie books that he's been reading that have told him about the contributions Italians like Galileo have made to the world. He then rattles off a litany of Italian American inventors, scientists, and other *prominenti* who contributed to Western civilization and asks,

> JOEY: How come I don't know this, Louie? How come nobody told me?
>   All they told me was about *The Godfather.* There's more important
>   things to read about than war. There are more important people than

generals. Nobody told me about other things I could have been . . . other things I could have seen myself as. . . . Don't you get it? We could have been these guys.[22]

Works like Vetere's *Gangster Apparel* join the fiction of Italian Americans such as Giose Rimanelli's *Benedetta in Guysterland,* Anthony Valerio's *Lefty and the Button Men,* Frank Lentricchia's *The Music of the Inferno,* Louise Ermelino's *Joey D Gets Wise,* and Don DeLillo's *Underworld* in creating a different future for the gangster figure in American culture, one that I suggest completes the maturity cycle of Italian American figures as they move from wise guys to wise men. Whether Tony Soprano represents a degeneration or a regeneration of the gangster remains to be seen, and actually is not as important as the fact that he has come to signify the postmodern American who struggles to fashion an identity that reconciles an ethnic past with a multicultural present. Perhaps it will be gangsters like David Chase's Tony Soprano who will lead the United States into a post-multicultural era in which Old World chauvinism will succumb to acceptance of New World diversity. But then again, society has always needed its tricksters and scapegoats, and Chase has created a contemporary trickster figure that serves that purpose well.

As Stanley Diamond tells us in his introduction to Paul Radin's *The Trickster,* "With the appearance of civilization, the concrete and ramifying image of the trickster becomes a segregated and vicarious aspect of human experience, acted out by the clown as an entertainment; and, at the same time, it is epitomized abstractly in the civilized assumption that evil, reified, befalls good men. Put another way, the concrete image of the trickster is suppressed, and simultaneously transformed into the problem of injustice."[23] It is from here that the gangster becomes the godfather, a patriarchal prototype left over from primitive southern Italian culture that resurfaced in the Little Italys that sprung up around the United States. Diamond recognizes this when he writes:

> Good and evil, creation and destruction—the dual image of the deity as expressed in the trickster—are fused in the network of actions that define primitive society. Therefore, moral fanaticism, based as it is on abstract notions of pure good, pure evil, and the exclusive moral possibility or fate of any particular individual—what may be called moral exceptionalism—is absent among primitive people. In primitive perspective, human beings are

assumed to be capable of any excess. But every step of the way, the person is held to account for those actions that seriously threaten the balance of society and nature."[24]

In the moral fanaticism of Anglo American–based culture, good and evil were separated, and as American man strived toward his notion of pure good, he had to be able to measure his progress by personifying evil in others. As Paul Radin remarks, "Only if we view it as primarily [psychological], as an attempt by man to solve his problems inward and outward, does the figure of the Trickster become intelligible and meaningful."[25] This is one of the functions of Tony Soprano—he figuratively embodies problems facing American society.

The trickster also works to help us organize our sense of community. Carl Jung saw the trickster as "[a] collective personification . . . the product of a totality of individuals and . . . welcomed by the individual as something known to him, which would not be the case if it were just an individual outgrowth."[26] The trickster, Jung writes, serves as a reminder of our shadow selves:

> The so-called civilized man has forgotten the trickster. He remembers him only figuratively and metaphorically, when irritated by his own ineptitude, he speaks of fate playing tricks on him or of things being bewitched. He never suspects that his own hidden and apparently harmless shadow has qualities whose dangerousness exceeds his wildest dreams. As soon as people get together in masses and submerge the individual, the shadow is mobilized, and, as history shows, may even be personified and incarnated.[27]

Jung sees trickster stories having therapeutic value: "It holds the earlier low intellectual and moral level before the eyes of the more highly developed individual, so that he shall not forget how things looked yesterday."[28] Observing gangsters can be therapeutic today.

Gangsters are the guys who at least try to bypass the system's acceptable ways of living. When they're successful, they give us all a sense of how things could be if we were outlaws; when they fail, they give us a sense of relief that it wasn't one of us. This is why the United States is obsessed with the gangster figure. He has become a modern trickster figure during a time when we have quite simply run out of types to play the trickster. In the hands of

American artists, and especially those of Italian descent, the gangster presents the last stand for traditional patriarchy in the United States and a chance for Americans to relive a known past as we head into an unknown future. David Chase's recovery of this dramatic figure in *The Sopranos* provides us with new insights into our situation high atop the junk heap of a postmodern consumer society that offers fewer opportunities than ever for us to reflect on the world we've created out of what was left by earlier inhabitants and reminds us that we need to pay more attention to the legacies we will soon be leaving for future generations.

"PA CENT' ANNI, DR. MELFI"

PSYCHOTHERAPY IN THE ITALIAN AMERICAN COMMUNITY

Michael Flamini

I was not always a book editor. For many years, I wandered halfheartedly through graduate school in pursuit of a doctoral degree in clinical psychology, learning to do psychotherapy in a variety of clinical settings, but always feeling happier in the company of English majors or browsing in a bookstore. It was a wrongheaded desire on the part of an only son to provide his parents with "a doctor in the family." It was a desire that was doomed to failure and, ultimately, came with a sting for my Italian American family: As part of my training, I was also required to enter into my own psychotherapy on the correct assumption that you can't teach someone to drive a car if you don't drive yourself. That therapy, of course, provided a light that would illuminate my wrongheaded choice of career path and show me the correct direction in which I should be going. It became my family's 300-pound gorilla. During one Christmas vacation, I dragged the beast home with me and finally invited him to sit at my parent's dining room table.

The announcement, to my mother and father, that I was actually in therapy myself was met with a very heavy silence during one of those pre-Christmas, "let's get all the difficult material out on the table so that we don't have to discuss it when the rest of the family arrives for Christmas Eve" dinners. If you're Italian American, you know the meal I'm talking about. The date is usually December 22 or 23. If you've been living away from home, mom cooks your favorite dishes and prods you to tell everything that's new in your life since Thanksgiving. I was in therapy long before Thanksgiving, but I swallowed that in silence, with the turkey and stuffing, about a month earlier. Now, though, I was ready to tell them and when I did actually say it—Uh . . . I'm in therapy . . . —my palms got sweaty, we all stopped eating, and the room contracted and expanded the way the hallway does in *Poltergeist* when Jobeth Williams is trying to rescue her children. I think my mother broke the silence with something on the order of "Why? What problems do you have?" My father, the more circumspect of the two, said something like, "So, pal, this is part of your training, right?" though clearly there were questions bubbling around in his head as well about exactly what I might be talking about with my therapist. The 300-pound gorilla was now sitting squarely on the plate of cutlets, picking at the bowl of spinach with garlic and oil. That's okay. He was welcome to them because, for once, the Flaminis had lost their appetites.

Now, while it is true that this is probably the reaction of most parents of any cultural background to a child's admission that he or she is in therapy, such an admission is surely even more problematic in a traditional Italian American family, because the spoken and unspoken cultural rule is that one never tells the family secrets outside the house for fear (as one of my aunts would have put it) of "making a shame" for the family. This rule of never telling the family secrets outside the house is central to understanding the allure of *The Sopranos,* because, not only are family secrets being told, but *Family* secrets—stories about Italian America's darkest secret, the Mafia—are being told as well. We watch each week for the new revelations that pour forth, both inside and outside Dr. Melfi's austere office. Understanding this taboo against telling family secrets outside the house is also central to understanding the reaction of the Italian American community to *The Sopranos.* The show reveals our Italian American family rituals, warts and all. It shows the country our family unity, but it also displays the darker, violent side of a segment of our community. The question that plagues us, though, as it has with every pop culture product from *The Untouchables* to the *Godfather* trilogy to *Goodfellas,* is whether or not what we are watching is defamatory and stereotypical. Does *The Sopranos* display any of the realities of Italian American life in the United States? Though I no longer practice psychotherapy, it is a process that still fascinates and haunts me. Tony's hours with Dr. Melfi have begun to obsess me with questions about what *The Sopranos* might mean for us, individually and collectively, as Italian Americans in the twentieth century.

Is Tony Soprano's entrance into psychotherapy so foreign to our culture? The Italian American community is not devoid of a culturally sanctioned method of unburdening oneself, but it is a method with an end result that is a far cry from psychotherapy. One of the most precious pieces of their homeland brought to the United States when the Italians emigrated was Roman Catholicism. Like the Irish before them, the church of Rome provided Italians emigrating to the New World with a cement for the new communities they would form in America. Long before Freud began developing "the talking cure," Roman Catholicism already had a cognate structure that provided, if not resolution, absolution: the sacrament of confession. In the Roman Catholic Church, if one wishes to receive the actual body and blood of Jesus Christ during the mass in the sacrament of Communion, one must be free of sin, and the only way to cleanse oneself is to confess to a priest in the ritual that begins "Bless me Father, for I have sinned." In contrast to the beginning of many therapy sessions wherein the therapist asks, "How are things this week?" the confessant begins with a breast-beating that is pretty much one-sided, until all the sins of the past week/month/year (well, some of us didn't go to confession that often) have been recited. At that point, the priest, who up until a few years ago was hidden behind a grille, recites the prayer of absolution and assigns the penance for those sins, usually a few Hail Marys (possibly a few Our Fathers if there's been some really egregious sin or he's in a bad mood) and sends you on your way.

Unlike psychotherapy, in which one sees the therapist, is allowed to vent in a free-form manner, and judgment never legitimately plays a part, confession has a rigid structure, always assumes the wrongdoing of the person confessing, and acknowledges the superiority of the priest listening to the confessor's sins. Ideally, therapy helps you to make sense of your life and those things you perceive as weaknesses or problems. It allows you to incorporate them into the picture you make of yourself and to get rid of or change those that trouble you. Confession tells you that what you've done is wrong, that there is no way to understand your actions other than as Sin, and that there is no real escape from or understanding of the dark parts of your life unless you acknowledge your wrongdoing, your dark heart, and participate in the endless cycle of sinning, confession, absolution, and penance. Therapy allows for the possibility of change, incorporating all parts of the self into a more functional and complex whole. Confession allows only for change if one absolutely and forever renounces sin, always keeping the idea in the back of one's head that humans will always sin and that there is no way of changing it. As my catechism teacher, Sister Canicia, put it, "Man [she was somewhat unenlightened with regard to gender issues] needs to make an outward sign of confession to show that he is truly penitent." In therapy, there are many paths to the inner self. In confession, there is only one path to Grace.

Therapy and confession do, though, have two important things in common. The first is a veil of secrecy that envelopes both the confessant's litany of sins and the therapy client's weekly concerns. Neither the priest nor the therapist is allowed to tell another person what transpired during confession or therapy. The other aspect common to both is that the priest and the therapist, most commonly, are not members of the patient or confessant's family. For Tony Soprano, both secrecy and family bonds are tantamount to survival. In visiting Dr. Melfi, he commits not one, but two major transgressions: First, he tells family (and sometimes indirectly, Family) secrets to "an outsider." Second, that person is, clearly, not a Roman Catholic priest. Instead of taking advantage of the culturally sanctioned sacrament of confession, Tony indulges in the foreign pastime of therapy with a female psychiatrist who is appropriately, and intriguingly, Italian American.

Tony's hours with Dr. Melfi pose other questions: How accurate is the depiction of Tony's path through therapy and how realistic is the response of his family? What intriguing things does *The Sopranos* have to say about the paths of Italian Americans through the somewhat culturally foreign thicket of psychotherapy? How does Tony's treatment with Dr. Melfi allow us a bigger frame of reference when thinking about the lives of Italian Americans in the twenty-first century, both in the way they see themselves and the way others see them?

Let's start with the presentation of Tony's psychotherapy. There is a small but growing body of psychotherapy research that looks at ethnic responses and attitudes toward psychotherapy among Caucasians of European descent. The most famous body of research in this area is the work of Monica Mc-Goldrick. Her *Ethnicity and Family Therapy* (1996), edited by McGoldrick with Joe Giordano and John Pearce, is still the bedrock people refer to when talking about ethnic groups in family therapy. Joseph Ponterotto and his colleagues have also contributed immensely to the question of ethnic group response to psychotherapy and have recently published one of the first articles dealing with the response of Caucasians of European descent to psychotherapy informed by quantitative research.

Early on, McGoldrick recognized the importance of variations among ethnic subgroups to psychotherapy, collecting her own work and that of others to provide family therapists—therapists who work with the whole family at once—with important cultural information useful to therapists working in different ethnic milieu. In the article on Italian families that appears in their *Ethnicity and Family Therapy,* McGoldrick and Giordano write, "For Italians, family has been the thread that has provided not only continuity in all situations, but also training to cope with a difficult world. *La via vecchia* [the old way] revered by Italians, symbolizes a value system organized primarily around protecting the family. While all cultures value the family, for Italians, family is an all-consuming ideal."[1] Hurting the family and telling secrets outside the family circle would be seen as ultimate transgressions of cultural rules formed in "the Old Country" and transplanted to these shores. The father is the undisputed head of the household, while the mother provides the emotional sustenance. Cross-sex ties between parents and children are evident, and one of the chief responsibilities of children is the care of their aging parents. Upward mobility causes children of these families difficulties as they are directly, or indirectly, bound both geographically and emotionally to their parents and reminded of their duty to take care of them in later years. The extended family members—uncles, aunts, cousins, nieces, nephews—are all expected to contribute to the family's well-being, owe nothing to "outsiders," and show respect, but not trust, to outside authority.

Such a family system has clear implications for family therapy. Most frequently, families of Italian descent will not appeal to an outside agent for help unless things have reached a crucial point. McGoldrick and Giordano suggest that a therapist can build trust with such a family by sharing common values, keeping questioning to a minimum, and recognizing that the father must not be threatened since his role is to maintain control of the family system. They warn against the avoidance of family members discussing "hot" issues by dancing around them. One of the most important things they discuss is the family secrets that help Italians maintain family boundaries. Frequently, these secrets contain information that is unimportant to the family system; however, the therapist is warned to tread lightly with such secrets for fear of damaging the family system, heightening mistrust, and creating further resistance. If one respects the power of the family, McGoldrick and Giordano suggest, family therapists can make great progress with an Italian family experiencing distress.

What, though, does the picture look like for individual Italian Americans seeking help from a social worker, psychologist, or psychiatrist? Oddly, there has been a dearth of research dealing with Caucasians of European descent seeking psychotherapy. One of the first, if not the first, article to begin addressing this issue with data gleaned from quantitative research was published by Joseph Ponterotto, et al.[2] Using a sample of 232 self-identified Italian American and Greek American undergraduate and graduate students in the northeast United States, the researchers administered a variety of testing instruments to determine the relationship between the level of acculturation among the individuals being studied and their attitudes toward entering psychotherapy. Acculturation was defined by using a definition developed by anthropologists over 60 years ago: "acculturation comprehends those phenomena which result when groups of individuals having different cultures come into continuous first-hand contact, with subsequent changes in the original cultural patterns of either or both groups."[3] If Livia and Junior Soprano's generation of *la via vecchia* represents the old, insulated, non-acculturated way of Italian American life in northern New Jersey, circulating only among "their own kind" at places like Satriale's Pork Store and St. Paul's Church, Tony and Carmela Soprano's life in the affluent suburbs of northern Jersey, circulating between shopping at the Short Hills Mall and brunch at The Manor, represents a more acculturated version of the Italian American lifestyle. Ponterotto and the other researchers wanted to see if there was any difference between the Livias and Tonys in terms of their reaction to psychotherapy. On the main issue of acculturation, the results were inconclusive; however, other results were tantalizing in terms of *The Sopranos*. Women had a greater recognition of personal need for counseling and more confidence in the potential usefulness and benefit of professional counseling services than did men. Regardless of gender, both the Greek and Italian Americans preferred a counselor with an ethnically similar background; however, if confronted with the choice of two different counselors, subjects placed more importance on a higher advanced degree, no matter what the ethnic background of the therapist. Women were wary of clergy members acting as help-givers or counselors, but both ethnic groups preferred family, parents, and other family members as help-giving sources for personal problems. What, then, does this research tell us about the accuracy of presentation when Tony Soprano engages in therapy with Dr. Melfi, and the reaction of his family?

As any therapist will tell you, the first session one has with the patient is, in many ways, the most important because you get a first look at the style of engagement the patient will use when interacting. The first episode of *The Sopranos* opens with a shot of Tony in Dr. Melfi's waiting room, staring up at the bare breasts of a Rodin-like statue. The fanciful suggestion is that this is the place where he will be infantilized again, sucking at the mother's breast while healing all wounds. However, these are stone breasts, unlike the ones he has known from the pole dancers at the Bada Bing Club or the young Russian women he sleeps with on his boat, *The Stugots*. The sustenance he receives from these breasts will be hard won. Dr. Melfi, impeccably tailored and wearing the coolest glasses this side of Nana Mouksouri, ushers him into her office. They to and fro about where he should sit and, when she asks about the collapse or panic attack that brought him to her, he responds that he's "Good. Fine. Back at work. [Pause.] Look, it's impossible for me to talk with a psychiatrist." From this, we know that Tony did not enter therapy willingly, corresponding to what McGoldrick has written concerning Italians entering therapy only as a last resort. He blacked out and, in the absence of any physiological evidence, he is referred to Dr. Melfi by his family doctor, Dr. Cusamano. One non-Mob-related Italian American ferries him across the river to another.

She asks him, "Any idea why you blacked out?" and he responds "Stress. I don't know. I've just been thinking that it's good to be in on the ground floor of something and I feel like I came in at the end when the best was over." He then relates an incident from the day he collapsed: His swimming pool had been visited for weeks by a family of ducks. Tony fed them to keep them returning. He once again tells her, "This isn't going to work. I can't talk about my personal life" and, at that point, Dr. Melfi stops him from going further. She draws an ethical line in the sand, telling him indirectly that she knows what line of work he's really in (when she probed earlier on his cue, he told her he's in "waste management") and cannot hear of any unlawful acts. She would, if she did hear of any such acts, be bound to report them to the legal authorities. She is firm but understanding and, thereby, implicitly asserts a cultural bond with him: I know what you do and, while I don't condone it, I won't judge you. She lets him know that the information came indirectly from another Italian American he trusts, Dr. Cusamano. With this assertion of a cultural bond between them, Tony begins to tell her more about his mother, and other family members like his Uncle Junior (he's also in "waste management"). The entire family begins to slowly enter Jennifer Melfi's consulting room, at that point. This bond between them seems to bear out what McGoldrick and Ponterotto have written about the importance of cultural bonding between therapist and patient as well as patient preferences for therapists of ethnically similar backgrounds. Not only is Jennifer Melfi Italian American, but she also has a degree in psychiatry from Tufts, satisfying Ponterotto's findings that an advanced degree is preferred when seeking a therapist.

He then returns to the episode of the ducks. Clearly, he is feeling more comfortable with her. He tells her, in a tender, emotionally laden tone, that on the day of his collapse, the ducks flew away, never to return—just like the glory days of "waste management." There is a pause. He changes course and begins to flatly describe horrors, in voice-over, which we see on screen; for instance, a man being badly beaten ("We had coffee . . ."). Like many patients in the early stages of psychotherapy, he makes a neutral statement that masks a deeper truth not yet ready to be revealed. One could also see this as what McGoldrick calls "dancing" around hot issues. He then stops and changes the conversation. He looks up at her diploma and says, "Melfi. What part of the boot are you from, hon?" And she says, "Casserta. My father's people are from Casserta." He says, "Avellino," and gestures with his thumb to himself. Another cultural bond between them has been asserted, and he says, "My father would have loved it if you and I had gotten together," in the first of many expressions of affection and erotic attraction that will pass between them in the episodes to come.

In a later session of episode one he says, "I understand therapy as a concept, but in my world, it does not go down." And in that admission, he seems to implicate the entire Italian American community beyond his family and Mob ties. She then prods him to talk about the ducks again and he leaves. He returns to therapy after another attack. She asks him if he has any qualms about how he makes a living, and he then skips sessions. They encounter each other in a Manhattan restaurant, where he thanks her for "decorator tips" and gets her seated immediately when her non–Italian American date could not. If one were giving this a purely psychoanalytic reading, one might say that his transference to her as male caregiver to the good mother begins to take hold. In the next session, he tells her about his dreams and he begins to discuss the ducks. He says, "Wild creatures came into my pool and had their babies. I was sad to see them go. I'm afraid I'm going to lose my family." Only then does she slowly begin the actual process of therapy. The bond of trust has finally been established between them and, before the first episode is over, he repeats to Artie Bucco the mantras she gives him as a salve for Artie's depression over losing his restaurant: "Talking helps. Hope comes in many forms." Tony is off and running.

Things move quickly in Tony's therapy. In fact, they move a little too quickly to be absolutely realistic, but face it, it would be terribly boring to watch an actual therapy, with its years of *longeurs* week after week. By the second episode, he is confessing feelings of guilt over his mother. (It took some of us years to get to that point.) In later episodes, Dr. Melfi brings him to the central recognition of the desire for mother love and, with the help of a little lithium, Tony experiences a fantasy. He "meets" a beautiful, young Italian woman, a dentistry exchange student named Isabella, who is taking care of the Cusamano's house next door. She is the idyll of pastoral Italy. She dresses in a white cotton slip that allows much of her to be seen while she hangs out the laundry. She sits under the same type of white canopy the Corleones sit beneath when Vito and his family return to Italy in *Godfather Part II* (Tony's favorite part of the trilogy). Her hair and face are straight out of an updated Sophia Loren fantasy. While talking to her over lunch, Tony's fantasy deepens and suddenly he is in Avellino, his family's town, in the form of an infant who is being coddled and nursed by Isabella. The fantasy is, in part, an interpretation of Tony's relationship with Dr. Melfi and, in part, one of the deepest for many Italian Americans: return to the Homeland. (As evidence of the strength of this fantasy, one might also mention a similar, albeit hilarious, return to the Homeland that the Ray Romano family made in an episode of their sitcom dealing with Italian American family life, *Everybody Loves Raymond*.) In the final and perhaps most unbelievable of their sessions from the first season, Dr. Melfi connects the dots a little too adroitly for Tony since she feels he's in danger. She pushes him to the realization that he has been telegraphing session after session: the feeling that his mother wants him dead and probably engineered the unsuccessful hit on him. She crosses a therapeutic line, and anger erupts between them with Tony overturning the coffee table, physically threatening her and, once again, ending the session. One might say that his transference is now being projected onto the bad mother. One might also just say that it's just plain old good television. At the end of the first season, however, he returns to warn her that her life is in danger. As she brought him to a realization, he returns the favor in the only way he knows how: He tries to provide her with protection.

Over the first three seasons, there are remarkable interchanges between the two of them. Some, like the famed "capicola incident," wherein Tony remembers the first time he witnessed his father's violent method of doing business (a revelation that seems to have most New York City analysis patients threatening their analysts with malpractice because they haven't had similar breakthroughs), are highly unbelievable; however, there are others that are quite believable, especially if one has been in therapy oneself. Some are touching and some harrowing. He tenderly touches her face as they have a therapy mini-session in her car after the aborted Mob hit. She stoically protects him from the knowledge of her rape in the third season, knowing his rage would be uncontrollable if he found out. He erupts and tells her that he hates pouring his heart out to a call girl. If one is to judge the reality of Tony Soprano's therapy with Dr. Melfi from these initial encounters, one would have to come to the conclusion, based on the research and writing from psychotherapists and researchers, that it has the ring of truth about it, even if some of the revelations are souped up to hyperspeed to satisfy a television audience. A Caucasian of Italian descent is forced into therapy after blacking out because there is no physiological basis for the event. He is wary of the therapist, saying that therapy is foreign to his world. The therapist is of the same cultural background, providing a bond. The patient dances around difficult issues, does not reveal secrets, and the therapist is sensitive to all of this, prodding only when necessary and only beginning the true work of therapy once a bond has been developed. Love, hatred, and intense transference/countertransference pass between them. Mob ties and the needs of television drama aside, what we see weekly does seem to match up with what experts in the field suggest can be expected with such a client.

Tony, however, is not the only person in the consulting room. What is the significance of Tony's psychiatrist being a woman? There is a long tradition in Italian American culture, as in many other cultures, of female healers from the same ethnic community being more acceptable than "outsiders." In his classic study of the Italian Americans in East Harlem, New York, *The Madonna of 115th St.* (1985), Robert Orsi talks about the healing women, springing out of the *comare* tradition, who are called in as a last resort to heal the sick. (The *comare* and *compari* are women and men who, though not related through blood ties, are considered trusted members of an Italian American extended family.) Women from this tradition not only act as healers, but they also assert the norms of the community, ensuring that the individual being cured does not move culturally outside of that community. Jennifer Melfi is a modern Italian American version of such a healer. Though she may frequently appear in black, it is more than likely a Giorgio Armani suit she's wearing than a traditional dress of mourning. She, herself, is enmeshed in a complex family situation. Her parents, like many of our parents, are well-meaning, non-Mob-related Italian Americans who know how to maintain cultural traditions without forsaking contact with the outside world. Her ex-husband, Richard, is a wan, WASP wannabe (though he'd never admit it) who pretends to embrace his Italian American culture but is actually ashamed of it. His shame stems from his inability to incorporate the reality of Italian American mobsters into the picture he's created of a sanctimonious Italian American community without stain. In a moment of frankness, Jennifer says to him, "In a world filled with poverty, starvation, ethnic cleansing and a lot of other horrible shit, you devote all of your energy to protecting the dignity of Connie Francis." Her son, who in a fit of pitch-perfect characterization is a student at Bard College, can discourse at length on the significance of Italian American gangster films in American culture, but he is so cleansed of his own ethnic background that he doesn't understand the slur inherent in the phrase "ginzo sauce." In a hilarious vignette, we are treated to a glimpse into family therapy with Jennifer, her son, and her ex. Their Jewish therapist (an interesting comment on their acculturated stance in contrast to Tony's choice of an ethnically similar therapist) indirectly rebuffs Richard, asserting his wife's ties to one of the great Jewish mobsters of the past, and even relishes it when he says, "Those were some tough Jews." If Jennifer Melfi brings Tony Soprano to a higher level of self-realization over the course of the show's first three seasons, he in fact helps her to delve more deeply into her healer persona and defend the complexity of her own ethnic heritage. In a later season, she further berates her husband for his own ethnic self-loathing as she suggests that his hatred of the Mafiosi is a smoke screen for his own uncomfortable stance with regard to his Italian American heritage. She correctly infers that it is Italian Americans like him who are so completely centered on the Mafia as a symbol of Italian American culture that they actually make it a self-fulfilling prophecy. Throughout the first three seasons of *The Sopranos*, Jennifer Melfi changes as much as Tony, deepening her relationship to Italian American culture, ultimately becoming one of those mythical seers every culture contains and cherishes. If there is any hero in this tale of north Jersey mobsters, it is certainly Dr. Jennifer Melfi.

How do both the family and the Family react to Tony's therapy? His wife, Carmela, is thrilled. Her reliance on the church makes her say that, while it's not a cure for his soul, it's a first step. Her acceptance of his therapy seems to bear out Ponterotto's data indicating that women in this group are more likely to accept therapy than men. On her own voyage of discovery, Carmela ultimately comes to distrust Father Phil, her spiritual advisor, again bearing out Ponterotto's findings regarding women and their attitudes toward turning to the clergy for help. When in a later season Carmela visits a non–Italian American therapist, the results are disastrous and she ignores the man's advice, preferring to stay within her own cultural boundaries and her own difficult, conflicted marriage to the Mob.

There is, though, another woman in Tony's life who is not so accepting of his therapy—his mother, Livia. A joyless harridan who is the archetypal *strega* of Italian folktales, she first hears of Tony's therapy from her grandson. She says, "Therapy. That's just a racket for the Jews," and goes on to deny that her son could be involved. "What does he need a psychiatrist for?" she wails. "He goes to complain about his mother." She intimates her knowledge to her brother-in-law, Junior (a capo in the Family), in the hope of striking back at Tony for placing her in a retirement community. McGoldrick and her colleagues seem to understand Livia and her relationship with Tony perfectly in their comments about cross-sex ties between parents as well as the child's duty to care for an ailing mother or father. When Junior says of Tony, "He's headed in the right direction," she says, "Where? Overbrook Mental Hospital?" When she finally tells Junior directly that Tony is in therapy she turns up the heat, suggesting he's telling Family secrets by saying, "God only knows what he says." The failed assassination attempt these two instigate is even, in part, fueled by her shame over Tony's therapy. While standing in line for a bargain movie matinee, she tells Junior that a cousin of hers who had a lobotomy would have been better off dead than going through psychiatric treatment.

For Uncle Junior, who actually organized the hit, the shame is deeper as he equates it with his own shame. Weeks earlier, rumors had circulated that Uncle Junior enjoyed performing oral sex on a woman he takes to Boca Raton. As this hurt his reputation as a capo, so too he feels would psychotherapy hurt Tony's. Both men are shamed by participating in acts that are seen as less than masculine. In the initial reactions by Livia and Junior, the creators of *The Sopranos* are suggesting that there is greater acceptance of psychotherapy among more highly acculturated Italian Americans of the third and fourth generations than there is among first and second generation Italian Americans clinging to *la via vecchia,* though there is no hard data yet to suggest it. Their wariness as well as Carmela's reaction to the non–Italian American therapist does, though, seem to bear out McGoldrick's statement that there would be suspicion of family members seeking other kinds of authority outside the family structure.

How does the Family react when they find out? For the purposes of this chapter, that's a less interesting question, because the evaluation would be pure conjecture. There is suspicion of Tony early on as he is followed by one of Uncle Junior's henchmen, but the assumption is that Tony has turned state's evidence. Tony tries to talk with Christopher about his depression, but he is shrugged off by Christopher's saying "I'm no mental midget. Take fuckin' Prozac? Not for this skinny guinea." When Tony finally does tell his crew about the therapy, the response is, surprisingly, more complex than one would expect. Paulie Walnuts admits to having seen a therapist for a period of time, though he later admits that it's difficult to accept that Tony's therapist is a woman. Silvio is a harder nut to crack, but he grudgingly admits, in another television-infused moment of comic relief, that it would be better if they could all talk with each other about difficult things. Their reactions make for good television, but there's really no way of knowing if this is how mobsters would react to hearing that one of their own was seeing a shrink.

Finally, if one is Italian American, one must ask what *The Sopranos* has done for us, if anything. Like therapists, we listen to it, react volubly to it as we watch and discuss it with our friends, as if they are therapists with whom we're discussing a difficult case. We personalize our relationships with the characters. Some of us love it and some of us hate it. *The Sopranos* is our generation's very own 300-pound gorilla. As *The Godfather* did for an earlier generation, it shows the outside world Italian American family traditions that we are proud of and want others to know about, telling stories that we love to chuckle over again and again, but also telling truths that we are afraid to reveal and confront. Ultimately, through the central depiction of Tony Soprano's therapy and its concomitant complications, *The Sopranos* puts the entirety of Italian American culture on the couch, connecting the darker side of our history with our family feasting, religious fervor, and dolce vita. We cannot hope to understand our culture, completely, until we, like patients in long-term therapy, accept a difficult truth about ourselves. To understand our dolce vita, our Italian American Ego so to speak, we must be honest enough to face the horror and ugliness of Mob history, our Italian American Id. In order to fully understand our lives as doctors, barbers, pharmacists, lawyers, beauticians, accountants, scientists, athletes, plumbers, dentists, writers, actors, nurses, professors, psychiatrists, and book editors, we have to incorporate into our cultural psyche *The Sopranos* and all its baggage because it is, like it or not, part of our heterogeneous Italian American community. Just as my parents valiantly accepted my own 300-pound gorilla to understand me as an independent adult, we have to invite *The Sopranos* into our understanding of our Italian American world. Let's return to the comparison between confession and psychotherapy and actually imagine Italian American culture itself as both a confessant and psychotherapy patient. One might say that, if Italian American culture was a confessant to the Roman Catholic sacrament of confession, we would see a culture leaving the confessional that would please Richard Melfi, because it would be a bland Italian American culture where all wrongdoing is expunged from the record. It would be an Italian American culture in a state of Grace, but one that would be, sadly, incomplete. In the vision of Italian American culture successfully completing psychotherapy, all the aspects of the Italian American community would be brought into the whole. The Corleones and the Sopranos would sit down with the Ray Romanos and Connie Francises, giving us something to measure each by in a more textured and realistic depiction of our world.

How will other Americans experience us, if we are to accept this dark side of our culture? It might be similar to experiencing a formerly neurotic friend who's been successfully through psychotherapy. Whereas we were comfortable with our friend's past neurotic behavior (though it may have occasionally driven us crazy), the new friend is stronger and more forceful, maybe making us just a little uncomfortable. With our Italian American neurotic defenses against the Mafia stereotype gone in the wake of a realization that this *is* part of our culture, other Americans might experience a stronger Italian American community unencumbered by its need to constantly deny or explain away its dark secret. By truthfully facing the Sopranos and their tradition, members of the Italian American community might become comfortable enough to say to other Americans, "Yes, that's part of my world, but not all of it. Get over it." Finally, we might be able to move on with our lives in a way that leaves no part of us behind.

At the end of Umberto Eco's *The Name of the Rose*, he writes, "One cannot truly know the rose without knowing its thorns." The same is true of Italian American culture: One cannot truly understand Italian American culture without understanding the Mafia. One need not embrace its legacy of crime and violence, but one must face it, understand it, and incorporate it into the view we hold of our community. This is something I'm sure Dr. Jennifer Melfi understands. We'd all do well to spend an hour or so in her consulting room every week. For the dose of reality she's brought to our community, I'd like to raise a glass of Chianti (*Riserva,* of course) and toast her with our wish for a long and successful life, "Pa cent' anni, Dr. Melfi."

CATHOLICISM, IDENTITY, AND ETHICS IN *THE SOPRANOS*[1]

Carla Gardina Pestana

The Sopranos and most in their circle are Catholic, naturally. The rhetorical query, "Is the pope Catholic?" might just as easily be applied to all the Italian Americans represented on television or film. Catholicism serves as one marker of Italian identity, and frequent references to it are made on this HBO series about Tony Soprano, a North Jersey Mafia boss, and both his biological family and his crime family. The show indeed represents a variety of Catholicisms, as different characters relate to the faith in various ways. Catholicism also carries with it the potential to confront the characters with the morality (or lack thereof) in their lives. The mobsters and their relatives grapple with the problems of religious hypocrisy, sin, and salvation when Roman Catholic moral teachings press in upon their participation or complicity in murder and infidelity.

For the Sopranos to be Italian Americans, they have to be Catholic, according to turn-of-the-millennium American cultural categories. Persuading an audience to believe in a community of non-Catholic Italians would be like trying to get them to accept a California without kooks. References to Catholic beliefs, images of devotional items, and the presence of priests all imbue the series with a sense of the traditional religious faith of most of the characters. This essentially Old World religion intertwines with the Mafioso lives of the principal characters, so that the religion and the livelihoods of the Sopranos are mutually reinforcing. The Soprano teenagers (and their entire circle) attend a Catholic high school. Anthony, Jr. (A. J.) receives confirmation, an age-old coming of age ritual that confirms his faith as a Catholic in a major ceremony. The requisite party at the family home follows this community religious event, where Italian food is prominently featured as another ethnic identifier. Carmela Soprano, Tony's wife, wears a cross; the medallion on the chain around Tony's neck could be that of a saint. In his mother's front yard a statue of the Virgin Mary in a grotto signals the family's Catholicism. A few homes boast crucifixes, although seldom in the traditional position in the bedroom. Carmela's bedside table is full of angels that look a lot like the statuary in my own family's Christmas-time manger scene. The dining room of Dr. Jennifer Melfi's parents is adorned with an imposing image of the Last Supper. Various people cross themselves. When a dancer in the topless bar where Tony Soprano and his associates gather crosses herself, she is shown only from the shoulders up as she does so, an editing decision that suggests a certain deference to the religious sensibilities of the audience. At the bedside of young gangster Christopher Moltisanti, the camera lingers on the medallion of the pope that his girlfriend Adriana La Cerva pinned to his sheet. Characters consult their priests. We witness the sacraments of confession (now also called "reconciliation") and the Eucharist (also known as "communion") in a bizarre scene in the Soprano family room. Catholicism is a frequent referent on the show, helping to establish the Italian American culture of *The Sopranos*.

Along with religion, pasta and language work as markers of Italian identity. The Sopranos and their friends do not speak Italian, but they use various Italian words, especially when discussing food or when swearing. I wonder if the ubiquitous epithet "fucking" ought not to be replaced with curses from Italy, although it is hard to come up with an all-purpose one to replace *The Sopranos'* favorite adjective. The Sopranos and their friends talk a lot about food. Carmela's relationship with her priest in the first season revolves largely around food. She thaws out trays of pasta to bake for him when he drops in to watch videos with her, and, when the family's pasta supply is depleted, other family members joke that he must have been around. Livia Soprano's baked ziti, a special favorite of Anthony, Jr., gets rave reviews. When his grandmother does not attend his birthday party, his disappointment centers not on her absence but on the missing pan of baked ziti, an entirely characteristic reaction for a fourteen-year-old boy. In my family, my mother's lasagna had a similar status, and my male cousins always asked whether she would be making it for family dinners they attended. (The secret was the use of Italian sausage; great lasagna cannot be made with ground beef. I have no idea what the secret to fabulous baked ziti might be.) The emphasis on pasta is in keeping with the lower-class status of most Italian immigrants to America. Only in the United States is pasta the centerpiece of an Italian meal, a custom that arose among immigrant families who could not afford the meats and fresh vegetables essential to the full array of Italian cuisine. Pasta is the mainstay of the Sopranos as well as a major indicator of their Italian heritage. Religion and pasta are strangely juxtaposed when Carmela walks in on her friend feeding the priest in the chapel of their church. Religion is one part of this package of referents that establish the identity of these characters as Italian Americans.

Based on my own experience, I would argue that *The Sopranos* does less than it could to create an authentic Italian American Catholic feel. Perhaps because David Chase, the show's creator, although an Italian American, was not raised a Catholic, the series lacks a densely Catholic environment.[2] Religious icons are particularly lacking. The set designers should have seen my grandmother's house: typical of many working-class homes in other ways, it was peppered with Catholic iconography. She had crucifixes, prints of the sacred heart of Jesus and of Jesus overlooking his flock, guardian angels watching over small children unconsciously avoiding grave danger, and, especially, images of the Virgin Mary. This iconography was ubiquitous. I was occasionally aware, when I brought non-Catholic friends over to her house, that they noticed these things. Only through their eyes did I even perceive their presence. Otherwise they were just a natural part of the environment, like the furniture. After my grandmother died, my family divided up her things, and I went home with three Marys and a Jesus. I then realized how many of these objects were routinely present in the homes of my older relatives. And now they are in my house, although less numerous and less prominently displayed. The home of Tony's mother should have been similarly crammed full of these types of objects, at least before Tony moves her to the nursing home. Carmela's suburban "McMansion" can be excused from this requirement, assuming that her upwardly mobile aspirations trump any tendency she might have felt to draw upon her own deep devotion in decorating her home. If the series' creators didn't want to buy all those objects, they could have borrowed them from descendants of Italian immigrants who each have at least three Marys and a Jesus at home.

Similarly, the show needs more rosaries. Many people in *The Sopranos'* world die or are hospitalized with terrible injuries, and their loved ones ought to be praying the rosaries at their coffins or bedsides. The first rosary to make an appearance on the show is well into the second season and is held by Livia, who is overreacting to the death of her daughter's father-in-law. There the rosary is a prop in a melodramatic, attention-getting ploy that causes Tony to roll his eyes. Yet every Catholic person on the show ought to own at least one—they are commonly given as gifts at first communions and confirmations as well as being heirlooms, many of them quite beautiful, that are passed down from one generation to the next. The comfort of this age-old meditative prayer might do some of these characters a world of good, and it would help to further establish their identity as Catholics.

And where are the saints? Neither visual nor spoken references to them are as frequent as one might expect. Livia refers to her ex-husband as a saint, but the viewers are given to understand that he did not by any stretch of the imagination fit that description. This false assessment of his character is self-serving, part of the way in which Livia complains about her present life. Livia herself ought to be conversant with and calling upon the help of actual saints, which would be typical for one of her background and age. Since she is such a monstrous character, supposedly patterned to an extent on Chase's own mother, perhaps he was loath to make her bear the burden of too much of the show's Catholicism.[3] If so, it is another indication of a certain defer-ence toward Catholic viewers. Adriana's use of a papal medallion to safeguard her wounded boyfriend is either a too subtle gesture intended to establish her theological naiveté (and such naiveté does run rampant in the Catholic com-munity as well as on the show), or a lost opportunity to use a more appropri-ate image at that moment. In the church at A. J.'s high school, the camera lingers for a moment on a statue of Saint Jude, the patron saint of lost causes and an especially popular saint in twentieth-century America, but the more usual panoply of saints is absent. If anything, *The Sopranos* could make more use of these Catholic icons in authenticating the cultural milieu the show aims to create.

References to religion, food, and language create an exotic cultural context in which to embed the Sopranos' story. Catholics, though they are the single largest denomination in the United States today, continue to be presented by the dominant culture of television and film as exotic and ethnic.[4] Film and television foregrounds Catholicism when characters are identifiably Italian American or Latino, but do not typically emphasize this faith when they are more assimilated. On this show the characters are mostly Italian, the Italians are all Catholic (or lapsed Catholics), and other Catholics are kept to a minimum. The only non-Catholic regular is the Jew, Herman "Hesh" Rabkin, who is in the inner circle of the Soprano crime family. Catholics other than the Italians are relatively thin on the ground. The Irish and their gusto in celebrating Saint Patrick's Day provide the context for Christopher's vision of hell: an Irish pub where it is always Saint Patrick's Day. When the two Russian thugs hired by Uncle Junior to scare Christopher cross themselves before pretending to shoot him, viewers probably think of Catholicism, although they are more likely to be Russian Orthodox.[5] Otherwise, in the series, Catholic is Italian and visa versa. These two components of identity are mutually reinforcing. The culture of the American media remains Protestant and WASPish (to the extent that it alludes to religion at all), in spite of the demographic reality of the United States. Catholicism gives an Old World flavor to characters, and references to saints and to Catholic rituals exoticize what might otherwise seem more mundane. Although the religion of almost any tradition includes elements that, if examined in detail, would seem exotic, foreign, and strange to the nonbeliever and especially to those of other cultures, popular presentations of Catholicism—a religion heavily imbued with symbolism and ritual—lend themselves to this sort of short-hand performance of the alien.

The Sopranos offers a number of good cases in point. When Carmela receives communion on the floor in front of the sofa from her priest in a late-night intervention, the actors recite much of the language of the Catholic sacrament. The odd juxtaposition of the communion ritual in front of an Emma Thompson video gives the whole scene a surreal quality that surprises us into focusing more closely on what the priest is saying. Ruminating on this imagery—so central to most of Christianity—brings out its strangeness. Even those of us conversant with the sacrament see it in a new way, and it is not hard to appreciate why non-Christians might think it cannibalistic. At a recent wedding mass of a cousin, the newly immigrated Chinese wife of another cousin audibly exclaimed, "Ugh, they are drinking blood!" during the Eucharist. Viewers can appreciate her shock when they observe Carmela taking communion in the family room, as the staging of the ritual in that setting renders it bizarre. Paulie's calculations of his chances of getting to heaven are equally strange, as they would be even to many modern American Catholics. This presentation of Catholicism sets an Old World or old-fashioned tone that shapes our understanding of the Mafioso culture as imbued with tradition.

By creating a sense of a culture steeped in ritual and tradition, the presentation of Catholicism gives a context in which to understand the crime "family" of Tony Soprano. Not only in *The Sopranos*, but also in many films about the Mafia, the presence of the ritual of Catholicism provides a sense of tradition. Even though both *The Sopranos* and *The Godfather* movies depict the criminal organizations in the United States as American creations, responding to American conditions, they are linked to the Sicilian Mafia in the popular imagination and in the realities created in the series and films. Just as the Church is millennia old, the Mafia seems an ancient institution, with an ethic that has deep roots in traditional culture. Valuing loyalty to one's crime family, even unto death, seems both quaint and appealing to many Americans, since American culture emphasizes the individual over the group and the present over the past. Living in a United States that is popularly viewed as lacking in profound commitment, an intense sense of community, and an appreciation of the past, audiences understand both the Catholic Church and the Mafia as representing all those things. Films about the Mafia have an enduring popularity because we are both repulsed and attracted by the ethic of that crime community. What is attractive in it, the Mafia shares with the Catholic faith that it is so closely identified with in the popular media.

Tony Soprano appreciates his family's Catholic identity largely in these terms. The Italian Catholic milieu that the show attempts to create not only establishes a context for the viewers but is also part of the characters' understanding of their own identities. For middle-aged Mob boss Tony Soprano, Catholicism is about identity, not personal faith. He reveres his heritage and traditions, referring to them frequently. An Italian American FBI agent evokes this common heritage to encourage Tony to cooperate with and trust him. His list of the components of their shared culture includes

Catholicism, here again a shorthand referent for Italianness. Tony's list may be a little different, but he thinks in similar terms—although he does not fall for the agent's ploy. On another occasion Big Pussy Bonpensiero tells A. J. that his heritage includes baseball and Catholicism, a pairing my own grandfather—though he would have disagreed with Big Pussy on many other issues—would have heartily endorsed. For his part, when Tony fantasizes an Italian past, complete with a dental hygiene student as Madonna figure, a church is prominently featured in his reverie. In a later actual visit to Italy there is no Catholic imagery. He and the female Mob boss visit the site of an ancient oracle and discuss malefic magic. Having exoticized Italian American Catholicism to such a great extent, the show's creators need some even more alien strangeness to set the Italian context itself. The powerful female figure of the gangster leader (who fears the misuse of her fingernail clippings and so has them burned) is almost a witch-like character. Never mind that the United States is full of believers in magic, even malefic magic. Here it stands for foreignness and helps to constitute Italy as an ancient and mysterious place.

Tony's identification with an Italian and Catholic heritage is accompanied by a lack of personal religious engagement. In the first season he is openly hostile to his wife's close relationship with the parish priest, and, as it turns out, for good reason. In one scene that illuminates his pride in his family's heritage, Tony goes with his daughter Meadow into a church. He says it has been a long time since he has been in this church (built by his ancestors, who were apparently skilled masons like a lot of Italian immigrants to America). We gather that it has been a long time since he has been in any church, except when family occasions like funerals or confirmations require it. He does fall into the routines and rituals of his childhood faith, absently crossing himself at the start of the prayers at the funeral service for his sister's father-in-law, while Livia wails at the back of the room. Tony seeks his redemption on the psychiatrist's couch, not in the pew or confessional of his family's religion. Exposed to existentialism by his son's own intellectual and spiritual crisis, brought on by the excellent education that Carmela and Tony are so concerned to provide their children, Tony asks his friend Pussy about Pussy's belief in God. He states his own doubts. He envies the Orthodox or Hasidic Jew who does not flinch when threatened. The Jewish man's religion, he enviously notes, gives him great inner resources that could help him to deal with his dangerous life of crime. Tony would like to have such confidence but he has not found it in his own religious heritage.

Doubt is one thing, a personal matter, and being identified as Catholic is very much a public matter, and one that is very important to Tony. Although his Catholicism is essentially superficial, he insists upon it for his family. So he can say to his son, "even if God is dead, you are still going to kiss his ass." During the same struggle, Carmela demands that A. J. "be a good Catholic for fifteen fucking minutes. Is that so much to ask?" The idea that A. J., with his sinful Mafioso father and his own existential crisis, would not be confirmed in the Church upsets both his parents. It violates his father's sense of family honor, his understanding of what it means to be a Soprano. This identification with Catholicism helps explain his ridicule of his sister's religion. Janice Soprano (or Parvati, as she initially prefers to be called) is Tony's older sister, who left home years before to escape their odious mother and create a new life on the West Coast. She there became a Hindu, modestly adopted the name of a major Hindu goddess and lived for a time in an ashram. Although *The Sopranos* has been accused of cultural stereotyping of Italian Americans, no one to my knowledge has complained about the stock way in which California and the West Coast are depicted. Tony dismisses Janice's suggestion that they all speak nice thoughts of their dead mother at her funeral as "California bullshit." As a native Angelena, I could point out that Janice did not need to leave New Jersey to join an ashram. In any event, Tony, who has difficulties in his relationship with his sister somewhat akin to those with his mother, scoffs at her religion. Nor does he fully understand it. When Carmela opines that it would not be Christian to kick Janice out of the house, Tony responds, "This shit works out. She's a Buddhist." Were we to call Tony on confusing a Hindu and a Buddhist, he would no doubt say it made little difference. At one point he derides his sister as "Vishnu come lately." He's ostensibly criticizing her for coming home only when their mother is ill after years of neglecting her, but his comment also makes light of her religion because it was recently acquired. Religions cannot be picked up in this way, in Tony's view. You have to live in the faith you were born into or do without. For Tony (and for others, such as his wife Carmela, who responds to a priest's contemptuous reference to "zany Zennies" by agreeing: "I could never just sit on the floor and think of nothing"), these alternate traditions and Janice/Parvati's effort to find solace from them is laughable. Janice affirms this to some extent at the bedside of her cousin Christopher when she declares that all the gathered family and friends need to pray for him. Old habits die hard, as they say. When she veers back toward Christianity, however, it is not to return to Catholicism but to take up a born-again faith that is held in equal contempt by her brother. Even if Tony finds no solace for his emotional and psychological troubles in his birth religion and envies Jews who do in theirs, he has no sympathy for his sister's search. Being a Catholic (even if only a lapsed or culturally identified Catholic) is, he feels, the only appropriate identity for a Soprano.

Tony's cultural Catholicism, laid alongside Carmela's devotion to the Church, suggests the range of Catholicisms that the series depicts. Tony and Carmela represent two extremes: he is lapsed and she is devout. That difference in part captures the tensions within their marriage. To some extent *The Sopranos* follows in the tradition of assigning to the women the responsibility for religion: women pray and thereby safeguard the family, while men live in the wider world, covered to some extent by the prayers of their womenfolk but not themselves prayerful. Robert Orsi describes such a dynamic among Italians in Harlem in the early twentieth century, but it was not limited to Italians or even to Catholics.[6] Tony is unengaged save on a cultural level. Carmela is fully engaged, and we see her pray, confess her sins, receive communion, and otherwise participate in her faith. For her, Catholicism is a guide and a hope, and she prays that her husband will return to the Church and find in it both of these as well. The wives in *The Sopranos*, like Carmela, mostly have a fairly uncomplicated relationship to their religion. Although one friend (Angie Bonpensiero) declares her intention of divorcing her gangster husband Pussy and scoffs at the religious arguments against doing so, most of the women seem devout Catholics, active in the church and guided by its precepts. A number of them fall into Carmela's habit of feeding and socializing with the young priest, Father Phil Intintola. Adriana, the girlfriend of Carmela's nephew, Tony's employee Christopher, shows little sign of belief until her boyfriend is shot and almost killed. Then she turns to her religious tradition as a source of comfort.

The men who are in the Mob have a more complicated relationship to the Church. Pussy claims to believe in God when questioned by Tony. Indeed he stands as A. J.'s confirmation sponsor and helps to deal with the boy's spiritual crisis. Tony suggests Pussy use a belt to beat A. J. into obedience, but

Pussy tries to talk him into participation, albeit on cultural more than spiri-tual grounds. Christopher jokes that the church building would collapse from the weight of his own sins were he to attend his cousin A. J.'s confirmation. Artie Bucco, although not in the Mafia, admits that he fell away from the Church in high school; like Tony, he expects his children to have a relation-ship to the Church, anyway. Paulie Walnuts believes fervently but superfi-cially. He thinks of the Church as offering spiritual protection against punishment in the afterlife, in a way analogous to the "protection" the Mafia offers to small-business owners in this life. When confronted with Paulie's ver-sion of Catholicism, Tony Soprano's doubt seems the more ethical and thoughtful position.

Along with Catholic identity, the ethical dilemmas raised by being in organized crime are a second major theme in *The Sopranos'* treatment of re-ligion. Most of the characters in the series are in the Mob or are related to those who are. Of the regulars on the show, only Artie and Charmaine Bucco are not involved in organized crime, and Charmaine worries that Artie's friendship with Tony will draw them into the criminal underworld. She would rather Tony and his business associates did not frequent their restaurant. Even Tony's psychiatrist, while strenuously avoiding any unethi-cal acts, feels implicated in his violent life as a result of what she learns through their therapy sessions. Actress Lorraine Bracco here reprises aspects of the role she played in the film *Goodfellas;* there she was a Mafia wife drawn to the criminality of her boyfriend's and eventual husband's life, whereas here she is a professional woman who feels a similar fascination for the evil acts committed by her patient. Those characters that are involved—directly or indirectly—in crime occasionally confront the ethical issues this raises for them. Carmela in particular grapples with the fact that she has ig-nored the nature of her husband's work while enjoying the largess that his criminal activity brings her and their family. Even some of the mobsters struggle with how to square their purported Catholicism with the murder and deceit they routinely commit in their work. Tony himself confronts this dilemma to some extent. Although thankfully most of the nation's 62 mil-lion Catholics are not in organized crime and do not carry the weight of these sorts of sins, these kinds of dilemmas—about the compromises with evil that everyone makes in their lives—are familiar to any Catholic viewer of the show.

The hypocrisy of being a Catholic and living the life of a mobster has been a recurrent theme in Mafia movies, for obvious reasons. The most powerful such moment comes in the baptism scene in Francis Ford Coppola's *Godfather, Part II.* In this scene, the new Don of the Corleone family, the youngest son, Michael Corleone, stands as godfather to his nephew. As in *The Sopranos,* when Carmela receives the Eucharist at home, the dialogue includes long passages from the Catholic rite, in this case the baptismal rite. As the priest intones, "Do you renounce Satan and all his works?" the visual image cuts to the murders of the heads of other crime families, a revenge killing for the murder of Michael's older brother Sonny. We see an impassive Michael Corleone agreeing to renounce sin, though he and the viewer knows that horrific acts are being committed in his name at the same moment. In one sense the film communicates the sheer hypocrisy of the life of the Catholic Mafioso. But the scene is more complicated than that. We know that Michael attempted to leave the family and that both he and his father intended another life for him. He attended college, was decorated as a war hero in World War II, and married a non-Italian (although apparently Catholic) woman. Only after the death of both his father and his elder brother did Michael come forward to take over the family's interests, and he did so vowing to his wife (with apparent sincerity) that he would get the family out of crime and into legitimate businesses. Watching him commit murder while vowing to renounce sin, we see this scene on a number of levels: he is doing what he is saying he will not do, but he also tried but failed to give up this life. An extremely powerful and affecting moment, it is also another example of using Catholic ritual to establish Italian ethnicity and Old World exoticism.

Compared to his counterpart in the *Godfather* films, Tony Soprano's estrangement from his family's religious tradition seems the more honest course. A lapsed Catholic, Tony apparently does not attend mass on a regular basis, although (like a lot of lapsed Catholics) he does attend for special family events. His lapsed status makes Tony far from unique—an estimated 16 to 20 million Americans are identified as non-practicing Catholics, making them one of the largest religious categories in the United States.[7] He doubts the existence of God, intrigued (as well as enraged) by his son's flirtation with existentialism. A poignant theme of the series involves the confrontation of Tony and Carmela's generation with ideas their children are exposed to as a result of receiving more and better education than their parents. Encountering existentialism, the Sopranos order their son to his room, as if they could hold back the force of European philosophical traditions with parental discipline. When the far better educated Dr. Melfi explains existentialism to her patient, saying that existentialists believe that the only sure thing in life is death, Tony finds this viewpoint to resonate with his own experience. He wonders whether life has a larger purpose, a purpose that is explained for Catholics by their belief in God, their efforts to lead a moral life, and their understanding that their actions on earth will dictate their experience in the afterlife. Tony lacks these convictions but has not found any other source of meaning with which to replace them. His lack of acceptance of his sister's spiritual search indicates that if he cannot find it as a Catholic, he is not going to find it at all.

For a criminal like Tony, the sacrament of confession creates a major stumbling block for participation in the Church. He avoids confronting the ethics of his lifestyle by staying away from confession, in which he would be called upon to examine his conscience and confess his sins. Ways around this conundrum exist for the wily and deceitful, of course. One of the boys who stole the communion wine in the church at the Catholic high school confides that he would confess to having stolen something but not to what it was he took. This scene suggests that the school requires that Catholic students participate in confession as well as mass, so that this boy was literally forced to confront how to deal with making some sort of confession without implicating himself to the school's priest. The boys, including A. J. Soprano, are caught, making the subterfuge unnecessary. Carmela accuses herself of doing something similar, when she tells her priest that she has not made a good (that is a full and frank) confession for some time. Her omission was presumably not as consciously chosen as that of the wine thief, which only suggests how easily one can avoid self-scrutiny and honesty on uncomfortable issues. Tony's strategy is different, because he simply stays away. He doesn't confront the dilemma of making a good or a bad confession, for he does not confess at all. But he is enough in the grip of his Catholic heritage to find some solace in the mock confession that is psychotherapy. The secular version of confession he has chosen in undergoing therapy has, from his point of view, the advantage that his psychiatrist is not supposed to tell him what to do about his activities. Whereas a priest would tell Tony to stop his life of crime and to undergo some form of penance to make amends for his sins, Dr. Melfi's mandate is to help Tony to cope better with the life he leads. Therapy may result in modifying his life in the interest of achieving greater mental health. Although the outcome might be similar—in that Melfi's suggestions might lead Tony to see that his work is psychologically damaging to him and so must be altered—from Tony's perspective, he retains control over any decision he might make at the psychiatrist's prompting. Such would not be the case were a priest to hear Tony make a full and frank confession. What sort of penance would a priest assign to a man with Tony's slate of sinful acts? It boggles the mind, although surely over the centuries the confessional has revealed sins as bad or worse.

Which is not to say that Tony does not struggle with the implications of his acts. He is more interested in justifying how he lives than in addressing the ethical issues that his lifestyle raises. He articulates a number of justifications for his criminal activities. He argues that all successful Americans are guilty of numerous illegal activities. Interestingly he suggests that Italian immigrant involvement in organized crime began in the United States and developed in response to the horrible labor conditions and lack of opportunity that confronted immigrants. Because the Rockefellers and Carnegies had cornered certain types of businesses, the poor Italians were left to pursue their interests in "waste management" and other marginal areas of the economy. Tony contends that Mafia members, although behaving much like other successful Americans, are reviled because of anti-Italian prejudice. The Tony Soprano character has been accused of encouraging this prejudice by his depiction of an Italian American crime boss; he enters into this cultural debate by offering his own interpretation of the dynamic between prejudice and his "business" activities. Other characters, including Dr. Melfi and her relations, debate the impact of organized crime on the image of Italian Americans as well. Tony also excuses murder by noting that everyone in his world knows the rules of it, has agreed to play, and realizes the consequences of breaking the rules. He also describes the players as soldiers, noting that it is acceptable to kill the enemy's soldiers in wartime. Tony is of course being duplicitous here, as not all those injured or murdered were willing players— the small-business owner forced to pay protection fees, for example. The fact that Tony feels compelled to justify his activities indicates some feelings of guilt about them. Perhaps his feelings of guilt are his best-developed Catholic trait. Should therapy cause Tony to confront the implications of what he has done, Carmela's priest hopes that it will lead him back to the Church. This is envisioned, however, as a two-step process in which therapy opens him to take responsibility and the Church then helps him to address the implications of his responsibility for the state of his soul and the sufferings of others. Though Tony is hurting, he is far from dealing with his life in these ways, so the justifications continue.

The Sopranos is full of sinners, and some characters use the Church to confront the consequences of their sinful lives. Carmela most directly addresses the relationship of her religion and her hypocrisy or complacency about her husband's life of crime. In the powerful scene on the floor of the den in front of the TV, she confesses to her priest that she has not made a good confession in a long time and that she has looked the other way about how Tony makes his money in order to have the nice house in the suburbs and send her children to a fine (Catholic) school. The confession scene itself is sexually charged, as she and Father Phil finally fall asleep in front of the TV, only to wake up with a kiss. This scene bears comparison to the *Godfather* baptism/murder scene. Roman Catholic rites make up a large part of the dialogue in both scenes, and both juxtapose sin and rituals of purification, whether baptism or confession. Yet Carmela's sins are domestic, having to do with sexual desire and the desire for worldly goods. Most viewers can presumably relate to her desires—for a sympathetic sexual partner or for a big house and fine things—more than they can with the desire for power and revenge that leads Michael Corleone to multiple and brutal murders. Carmela's sacraments and her temptations occur in the home, in front of the TV. Although HBO claims "It's not TV. It's HBO,"[8] the prominence of the television set in the scene has a self-referential quality that is similar to the many allusions the gangsters make to their favorite Mafia movies. Unlike her husband's (whose crimes are more in line with Michael Corleone's), Carmela's sins can be viewed with some sympathy. Although she is far from goodness, she perhaps comes closer to it than any other character on the show.

Like a lot of good Catholics, Carmela both reveres her priest and can see beyond his individual foibles to the Church as a transcendent institution. The first season ends with Carmela accusing the priest of taking a perverse pleasure in cultivating close relationships with spiritually needy, lonely women. Not only Carmela but also many of the women in her circle are close to Father Phil, often feeding him pasta and confiding in him. He is also implicated in the sin of enjoying Tony's largesse without thinking too deeply about where it comes from. Knowing the source of Carmela's wealth does not stop him from accepting her donations, her help with fund-raising, and her hospitality—especially pasta and a chance to watch Emma Thompson on video. Carmela's world is full of men who have compromised themselves, and she struggles to free herself from her own complicity in their actions. After the moment of intimacy when they fell asleep watching videos, she realizes that Father Phil is titillated by his relationship with Church matrons: he likes intimate but ultimately chaste relationships. After she speaks her mind to him, he disappears from the show for an extended period. As a result, we have no idea if he heard her and changed his ways in response to her accusation. His purpose was to give Carmela the opportunity to make some realizations about her own loneliness and her complicity. Learning from him, she is then ready to move on. Rejecting Father Phil, however, does not lead Carmela to a spiritual crisis. She remains a devout Catholic, understanding his weakness as simply human and not a reflection on her beloved Church. When she tries later with a different priest to get advice about her complicity in her husband's crimes, she is told to enjoy that portion of Tony's earnings that are not ill-gotten. Carmela observes that "the Church has changed so much," but we can wonder whether she is correct on that score.

If confession is the nodal point in Tony's relationship with Catholicism, the Church's position on divorce represents a major point of contention for Carmela. Carmela is trapped in a dilemma faced by many Catholic women. Her husband is egregiously sinful and corrupt, to the point that removing herself from the marriage might seem an act of moral purification. Yet her faith, with its prohibition on divorce, tells Carmela to remain in the marriage. As she tells her friend Angie Bonpensiero, "marriage is a sacrament. The family is a sacred institution." When she delivers that line, Carmela is struggling with her commitment to her own marriage. Besides his nefarious activities, Tony keeps a mistress and goes to prostitutes; his idea of being a responsible husband is having his mistress screened for HIV. Carmela has met a wallpaper-hanger who symbolizes to her a good husband. He stayed by the bedside of his wife all through her torturous death from cancer and has not yet recovered. She fantasizes about such a husband. Trying to persuade herself to remain in her own marriage, she urges Angie not to forsake hers.

When Carmela points out that the Church opposes divorce, Angie quips, "let the pope live with him." As it will turn out, Tony himself releases Angie from her marriage, after he discovers that her husband has been talking to the FBI. But for Carmela, the dilemma remains. Being a good Catholic by forswearing divorce means she must remain in a marriage to a troubled and unfaithful man with extensive criminal dealings. Annulment, although it might be possible in her case, is difficult to obtain and might well, to a woman of Carmela's perspective, seem as much a mark of failure as divorce would be. Tony's marriage is held together in no small measure by her conviction that it would be sinful to end it.

Although Tony's part in their marriage is ignoble by almost any standard, he embraces Carmela's values (yet applies them only to his life within the Mafia). Tony's other family receives the loyalty and commitment that Carmela accords their marriage. Just as in Carmela's Catholic commitment to marriage, Tony feels irrevocably committed to his crime family. Once in the Mafia, it is not possibly to leave. If a member is caught attempting to leave, he will be killed. This is most poignantly the case with Big Pussy, Tony's dear friend and A. J.'s confirmation sponsor who is also a snitch for the FBI. While Big Pussy works toward what might be characterized as the Mafia equivalent of an annulment (getting into a Witness Protection Program), his crime family doles out the ultimate punishment. When Tony, on a college campus tour with his daughter Meadow, encounters a snitch who fled punishment by the Mob, he kills the man. According to Tony's code, no one is allowed to leave. Carmela's attitude toward the sacramental vows of marriage is similar to that of the Mafiosos toward their oaths: both are inviolate. Merely questioning either shocks the devout Catholic wife or the committed Mafia man. Loyalty and tradition for Tony are focused above all on his crime family, while for Carmela the focus is on her marriage and the family that resulted from it. The life Tony leads with his crime family causes many of the ethical dilemmas that Carmela experiences in her marriage. Hence their two value systems are at once quite similar and very much in conflict.

Carmela abandons her usual religious passivity toward her husband's work in a dramatic moment in which she intervenes spiritually to save her nephew. With Christopher in surgery after receiving severe gunshot wounds, Carmela retreats to an unused hospital room to pray for him. She prays not only for his survival but for him to be granted vision to see, in effect, the evil of the criminal lifestyle that he, her husband, and many of the others gathered in the hospital to await the outcome of his surgery all share. When Christopher is brought back to life after having died momentarily, Carmela believes that her prayers have been answered and informs Christopher that he was saved so that he could do good for himself and the others. The depth of Carmela's faith and the solace it provides her is readily apparent in this encounter, making her the major exemplar of the devout Catholic in the series. Her emotional breakdown before the painting of baby Jesus carries a similar message.

Other characters are also driven to confront their spiritual circumstances after Christopher's near-death experience, in an episode packed with Catholic overtones. At the moment when he briefly dies, Christopher has the classic vision of death, with a tunnel and a light. When he arrives at the light, however, he finds a bouncer guarding the gates of what he takes to be Hell, which seems to be an Irish pub on Saint Patrick's Day. There he receives a cryptic message for Tony and his capo, Paulie Walnuts, from his deceased father. Tony at least feigns unconcern over this, although his questioning of Pussy about the existence of God belies his nonchalance. What motivates him to lie to his wife, describing the vision as featuring Jesus and Christopher's deceased father in Heaven? Perhaps he simply wishes to shield her from the thought of her cousin (Christopher's father) in Hell. Or perhaps he intuits that she would see him as the sinful father, with the same fate awaiting him. Does he want to comfort Carmela that such will not be the case, or shield himself from her interpretation of the vision?

Paulie's reaction reveals a folk Catholicism that sees adherence to the Church as a spiritual investment. He decides that Christopher visited not Hell, but Purgatory. This possibility is clearly a comfort to Christopher, who can hope that his father will someday be relieved of his agony. With the senior Moltisanti's punishment so much in the spirit of Dante's *Inferno,* viewers may well question Paulie's reinterpretation. Paulie explains his understanding of Purgatory in a way that would make any dead Catholic theologian spin in his grave. It is also an understanding that will be familiar to many, non-Catholics as well as Catholics. The Catholic doctrine of purgatory allows for the forgiveness of sins after death. A person who dies in a sinful state (without having received the sacrament of Extreme Unction for the forgiveness of sins at the time of death) may be saved from eternal damnation by prayers for the dead and other means. Popular belief envisions Purgatory as a place where people are sent for a period of time depending on the extent of their sins. The pope recently reiterated that Purgatory is a "condition of existence" rather than a place.[9] Paulie believes otherwise and has constructed a spiritual economy designed to deal with this place called Purgatory. He has carefully tabulated all his sins, and he has a formula for calculating how many years he will be spending in Purgatory. The formula is fifty years for each mortal sin and twenty-five for each venial sin, so his tabulation condemns him to just six hundred years in purgatory. (At least as I was taught, mortal sins, involving turning away from God, cannot be absolved in Purgatory.) He opines that six hundred years will seem a mere drop in the bucket of eternity.

Any viewer watching Paulie in action for even a few episodes has to conclude that he either spends a lot of time in confession and has absolved himself of many of his transgressions or that he is grossly undercounting his sins. Even according to his own system, we might expect him to spend far longer in purgatory than he anticipates. Paulie's economy of sin and salvation, although not based on official Church teaching, is representative of a folk tradition within the Church. The idea that one can do penance and be absolved of sin has led some lay Catholics to believe they can sin freely and then "buy" their way out of the punishment with penance or time in Purgatory. Non-Catholics occasionally criticize the Church on the assumption that this is its teaching, and some lay Catholics encourage them in this view. I have never heard any Catholic state the proposition in quite the bald terms employed by Paulie, but then to the best of my knowledge, I did not know anyone in organized crime in my childhood. One of my older relatives was told that attending mass on a specific day of the week for a certain number of weeks or years would protect her from eternal damnation were she to miss receiving the deathbed sacrament of Extreme Unction. This pre–Vatican II practice was apparently widespread, and it partakes in a less egregious way of the sort of economy upon which Paulie is pinning his hopes. It offered a sort of insurance policy for the devout, although the presupposition was that the faithful would continue to try to live by the Church's teaching throughout their lifetimes. Paulie takes this sort of arrangement to mean that he can do as he pleases and he will be safe in the end. His convictions about Purgatory, although somewhat exaggerated, do point to a (mis)understanding about Purgatory that resonates with some Catholics of his generation.

Paulie's spiritual economy offers him coverage not only through the existence of Purgatory but also in the benefits of charitable giving. Despite his apparent insouciance, Paulie is unable to hold his fears at bay after hearing Christopher's message. Unlike Tony, Paulie does not even feign unconcern. He in fact becomes obsessed with the vision and its meaning, and he begins to be haunted by his murder victims. He experiences extreme anxiety, and his girlfriend counsels him to visit a psychic. Finally he ends up with his priest, to whom, the priest asserts, he ought to have turned in the first place. Paulie reacts to his fears by lashing out at the priest, berating him for his own troubled psychological state. Here again he reveals another component of his salvific economy. Because he has made ample donations to the Church, Paulie believes that his conscience ought to be clear. Thoughts of his murder victims ought to be wiped away as a result of his charitable acts. He takes absolutely no responsibility for what he has done and experiences indignation that he feels bad about it despite his contributions. He clearly thinks of the Church as analogous to the Mob—he pays for protection and expects to feel safe. Church charity is thus for Paulie an insurance policy; he can do as he likes and as long as he pays the protection he will not suffer the consequences of his actions. It's a theologically naive position, but not a completely outlandish one. Surely some Catholics over the millennia have thought of their pious works in the same terms, and some aspects of Church belief, such as penance for sins, might be seen as encouraging such a view. Of course Paulie demonstrates no intention of repenting his sins, which would require some resolve to change his ways, and thereby avoids confronting what he has done, much less trying to stop doing it. Paulie has worked out a system whereby he can remain Catholic and remain a Mafioso, in which the former identity covers him for the sins of the lifestyle involved in the latter. He knows there are ethical objections to "whacking" people, but he assumes he will be ultimately forgiven. From his own perspective, Paulie is as devout as Carmela, though his faith facilitates rather than discourages his sinful life.

The Sopranos has been accused of encouraging prejudice toward Italian Americans. It is the case that most representations of Italian Americans in popular culture focus on the figure of the Mafioso. The sum total of images purveyed equate being Italian with being in the Mafia. The truth is that modern American culture is not much interested in Italians, but it is fascinated with the Mafia. The film *Moonstruck,* which portrayed honest Italian

Americans who carry all the same religious and culinary identifiers as the Sopranos, offers an isolated exception. This cultural fascination fuels the creation of numerous films and now this television series on Italians in organized crime. Considered on its own terms, *The Sopranos* depicts the life of its characters, religious or otherwise, in fairly authentic terms. Many characters, Tony among them, feel a fierce pride in their Italian heritage and its Roman Catholicism. When the Melfi clan debates the damage that the Mafia does to the popular image of Italian Americans—in a scene that references the show's reception—the mention of Mother Frances Xavier Cabrini, the first American saint, captures this sense of ethnic pride. It also indicates the way in which this pride and identity are partly tied to religion. The commitment to continuing the family's association with the Catholic Church across the generations—even among those with tortured or attenuated personal relationships to the Church—is quite realistic.

For all its foul language, murder, and infidelity, the series treats Catholicism with a degree of respect that is surprising. The Church, like every other serious topic touched on by *The Sopranos,* is sometimes played for laughs. Even as *The Sopranos* pokes fun at the sacred, it also takes it seriously. Sometimes the evidence for respect is indirect, as in the choice not to show the bare breasts of the stripper as she crosses herself before the television that reports the death of acting family boss Jackie Aprile. But often *The Sopranos* tackles the ethical dilemmas of sin and salvation. It explores how to live the life of a Mafioso or a Mob boss's wife while also living with one's conscience and one's God. The characters, for all their egregious acts, are rendered sympathetically. This portrayal of the likeable murderer is part of what makes the show so provocative and troubling. But by humanizing these people in a way that has not been done in any treatment of the Mafia in the popular media to date, the show also allows us to appreciate their personal struggles. They are anxious and fearful. They worry about the existence of God and the state of their souls. Their relationships to the Church cover a wide spectrum. Paulie's calculating Catholicism depicts a folk version of that faith at its worst, but Carmela's more self-reflective and informed faith offers a version with more integrity. Perhaps the very best Catholics don't live in *The Sopranos'* world. But the Catholics who do inhabit it are recognizable. In their humanity and their striving they even occasionally win our respect. And, as the popular media has schooled us, respect is highly valued in this culture.

IF SHAKESPEARE WERE ALIVE TODAY, HE'D BE WRITING FOR *THE SOPRANOS*

George Anastasia

In the early 1950s my family moved from a row house in an overwhelmingly Italian American neighborhood in South Philadelphia to a small, suburban community in Southern New Jersey. We were pioneers in what became a twenty-year migration that would change the face of America's older cities. Our arrival was greeted with mixed reaction in the largely white, WASPish middle-class community in which we settled.

Our next-door neighbor, a cantankerous old man who was one of the original homeowners on the block, allowed as how my father didn't seem to be too bad a guy "for an Italian." My father was a World War II battle-decorated Marine who brought his young family to the suburbs in search of the American dream. His parents had come to this country from Sicily. He was the youngest of seven children and the only one in his family to have graduated from high school. He shrugged and ignored the old man.

My mother, who was only half-Italian, was less forgiving. And when an unsigned note found its way to our mailbox, she took the offensive. The note, as I recall, made some reference to "South Philly wops" who weren't wanted in the neighborhood.

I was four years old. My mother was pregnant and would soon give birth to my sister. A younger brother would follow. I don't remember much about that time except the absolute truth that my mother instilled in me.

"Just remember," she said. "There are two kinds of people in the world—Italians and those who want to be." Then we talked about Joe DiMaggio and Rocky Marciano and Mario Lanza and Frank Sinatra. We even discussed Al Capone.

"Italians are the best at whatever they do," my mother would say. "The best singers, the best athletes. They're even the best crooks."

Later I would learn about La Guardia and Montessori and Marconi and Galileo and Dante and Brunelleschi and I would add them to my list. Sure, it was chauvinistic. Eventually I realized there were no absolute truths. Not everyone wanted to be Italian. But it was that attitude, instilled at an early age, that was my defense against slights, real or imagined, that came my way because of my ethnicity. I carry it still. If someone doesn't want to deal with me because I'm Italian, if someone doesn't want to associate with me because of my heritage, that's his or her loss, not mine. I was not raised to be defensive about who I am.

It's funny now when I think about it. Most of this came from my mother rather than my father. He never said much about what he or his parents had gone through. But he did say this: "You have to like who you see when you look in the mirror each morning."

He knew who he was.

I think *The Sopranos* is a good, sometimes great, television show. It's well acted, well written and, most weeks, dead-on accurate. It doesn't bother me that the characters are Italian Americans and mobsters. It's a drama. It's a story. Organized crime is the backdrop. It's the vehicle used to drive the narrative. Tony Soprano is Everyman. He has problems. He struggles, sometimes in unusual ways, to deal with them. Sometimes he succeeds. Sometimes he fails. Millions of viewers tune in each week because they care what happens. That's why the drama works.

King Lear offered the same kind of attraction. You think you've got problems, look at this guy. And he's the king of England, for crying out loud. If it's *Mister Lear* the play closes in a week.

Think about it.

If you don't like *The Sopranos,* and that's certainly your right, change the channel. But please, stop whining. I'm more offended and embarrassed by the portrayals of Ray Romano's mother and father in the hit sitcom *Everybody Loves Raymond* than I am by anything David Chase has offered in three years of his Mob saga. But I'm not going to wrap myself in the Italian flag and scream about being a victim of the insensitive, uncaring, profit-driven entertainment industry. I just don't watch the show.

How would African Americans react if they were portrayed in such a negative way, members of the Italian American groups that are complaining about *The Sopranos* often ask? Hello? Have you been watching television? Have you gone to the movies? How many black perps have been arrested on *NYPD Blue* during the long run of that highly successful series? Does the viewer assume that because one black is portrayed as a drug dealer, all blacks are drug dealers? How about George Jefferson? Was there ever a bigger buffoon on a television sitcom? On two, actually. Was George Jefferson a positive role model for African Americans? Should he have been?

This is television. Not for nothing is it called the boob tube. Occasionally, there's a drama or a sitcom that connects, that rises above the mundane and is actually entertaining or, better yet, thought-provoking. *The Sopranos* sometimes fits that description. So did another television show on which David Chase clearly left his mark. It was called *Northern Exposure,* and for my money it was one of the best-written pieces of hour-long drama ever to appear on TV. *Northern Exposure* was full of references to literature, philosophy, and history. They were often thrown at the viewer in a whimsical fashion. The assumption was that the viewer would get the reference. If you did, fine. If not, too bad, because the story was already moving in another direction. It was fun. It was entertaining and challenging and sometimes downright erudite. The characters never talked down to the viewers. I find some of that in *The Sopranos* as well.

But by and large, television is brain pudding. It lacks substance.

Karen Abbott, a reporter in Philadelphia writing about the hypersensitivity of one of these Italian American groups that purports to speak for all Italian Americans, said it better than I could. In an article in *Philadelphia Weekly* she pointed to a survey the group had referred to in one of its press releases complaining about the stereotyping of Italian Americans by the media and entertainment industry. The survey supposedly found that "three of four Americans believe that Italian Americans are associated with organized crime" because of shows like *The Sopranos*. Abbott then noted that if you followed that logic you could assume that "during the height of 'Happy Days,' three of four Americans thought Italians could turn on the juke-box with a jab of the elbow."

Arthur Fonzarelli, positive or negative portrayal of an Italian American on television? Lt. Frank Furillo of *Hill Street Blues?* Baretta? Columbo? How about the movies? *The Godfather, Parts I* and *II* (*Part III* is not worth discussing). Classics or cheap shots? *Moonstruck? Marty?* The original *Rocky? Raging Bull? Goodfellas? A Bronx Tale?*

How about *Good Morning Babylon?* Not a great film, but one with a defining moment that said it all. The central figures in the movie, two young Italian immigrants, one played by Vince Spano, have made their way to Hollywood in the early days of the film industry and are working as carpenters for a set designer. In one scene, the foreman berates one of the Italians, asking him who he thinks he is. The other Italian comes to his friend's defense. (And here I am paraphrasing.) "We are the sons of the sons of the sons of Michelangelo, Dante, and DaVinci," he says. "Who's son are you?"

They knew who they were.

Cut through all the sound and fury surrounding the arguments for and against *The Sopranos* and it comes down to that. We know that all Italian Americans are not gangsters. I guess what some people have a problem getting past is what I consider a given: Most Americans, at least those with any kind of intelligence, know that as well. Only bigots and idiots buy into stereotypes and I don't think we need to waste a lot of time and energy worrying about them. They also believe all Jews are rich and all African Americans lazy.

Are we, as Italian Americans, so insecure about our position in society that we believe a television show could somehow negate all the accomplishments over the centuries that can be attributed to Italians and Italian Americans? I don't get it. I don't understand how anyone can think this way. My position is basically this: Any ethnic group that can give America Anton Scalia and Camille Paglia in the same generation doesn't have to worry about Tony Soprano being its poster boy.

Maybe it's a generational thing. Maybe I don't feel the same way because I've benefited from the fight that was fought by my father's generation and his father's. They were the ones who came face to face with the anti-Italian prejudice and paid the price in lost opportunities and second-class citizenship. But I look at Scalia and Paglia and Lee Iacocca. I look at Rudy Giuliani and Geraldine Ferraro and Mario Cuomo and Martin Scorsese and Francis Ford Coppola and Madonna and Robert DeNiro and Al Pacino and I say, Where are the doors being slammed in our faces? Where are the opportunities being denied?

People are fascinated by and attracted to *The Sopranos* for many different reasons. Part of it has nothing at all to do with ethnicity and part of it is entirely because of ethnicity.

Americans have always been beguiled by outlaws. Billy the Kid and Jesse James were icons long before Al Capone or Vito Corleone. There is something about the rogue that strikes a chord with the American public. There is a strange, distorted, Bonnie and Clyde romanticism that allows the public to identify with the independence of the characters even while being put off or offended by the violence and criminality.

Ethnically, there is also some truth in the maxim of my mother. There are many people who wish they were Italian. Or wish, at least, to have a clear sense of who they are, a clear idea of their roots and their heritage. The melting pot is wonderful in many ways, but over four or five generations, it can also suck the life, the personality, out of an individual. It is, perhaps, egocentric and certainly, again, chauvinistic, but I think American ethnics—Italians, Latinos, Jews, those groups that celebrate their culture and recognize its value—have more fun. They seem to understand what it means to embrace life. There are other Americans who envy that, who want to partake, even vicariously, in that celebration. *The Sopranos* allows them to do that. And that doesn't bother me in the least.

If the stereotype of an Italian American is someone who wants to grab life with both hands, someone who loves to eat good food, loves to spend hours with his extended family, someone who's not afraid to show emotions, I can live with that. And if that character is a mobster or a detective or a sportswriter, what's the difference? It's about who they are, not what they do.

I have a favorite restaurant in Philadelphia. It's called Pizzicato. It's a small Italian bistro. Very New York. The young waiters and waitresses all dress in black. The menu is not extensive, but the food is great. One of the first things the waiters or waitresses will do, after taking your order, is come over to the table with a bottle of extra virgin olive oil and a loaf of crisp Italian bread. The bread, when dipped in that fantastic oil, is heaven, but it is impossible to eat without making crumbs. It's messy, but it's wonderful. So is being an Italian American. It's an inexplicable fact of life, and one that I think the people who complain and whine about *The Sopranos* have either forgotten or never understood. There was an episode in the second season, I think, that made a reference to this group. Tony Soprano called them "Wonder Bread Wops." They don't like crumbs. They prefer white bread with margarine. It's very American, homogenized. It's not messy. It's neat, safe, bland. It has no flavor.

There was another episode in which Tony Soprano tried to explain what it meant to be an Italian, how it was different. He talked about honor and family and loyalty. His sense of that is certainly distorted, which is the point of the drama. But then that's what the Mob, the Mafia, Cosa Nostra, is all about. This is a criminal group of Italians or Italian Americans who have taken all the positive values of the Italian experience—family, honor, and loyalty—and bastardized them to justify their own behavior.

"Omerta" (literally "to be a man") is the time-honored, but increasingly ignored, code of conduct to which all Mafiosi supposedly adhere. A man takes care of his own problems. A man is responsible for his own actions. A man places his family above all else. A man would give up his life for those he loves. Those are strong, noble, sensuous values. And they hit upon a theme that is often lacking in American society in general. We Americans have more than enough to do, but too often we struggle with what it is we want to be, with who we really are. Identity can be found in honor, family, and loyalty. From *The Godfather* through *The Sopranos,* writers have used the Mob to offer a glamorized sense of those values. It is a nobility that may not exist in real life, but it is a nobility that is none the less attractive to the viewer or the reader.

Two years ago I wrote an open letter to David Chase to mark the start of the second season of *The Sopranos*. I'd like to expand on that here as the fourth season is about to begin.

August 1, 2002
To: David Chase, producer and writer
From: George Anastasia, Philadelphia Inquirer *Mob reporter*
Re: The Sopranos

Yo, Dave.

A couple of the guys from downtown wanted me to let you know how much they were looking forward to the next season of The Sopranos.

"Tell 'im he really nailed it," one of them said to me the other day over lunch.

It's not the first time your show has come up in conversation. Tony and Uncle Junior are favorites with the guys I'm talking to. They also like the fact that your wiseguys have lives away from the office, so to speak.

Most of them have wives, girlfriends and mothers. The combination makes for a lot of headaches.

Agita.

I don't need to tell you.

They used to think Tony's mom, Livia, was a bit of a stretch, but they were willing to go with it. I tried to explain the "Caligula" and "I, Claudius" thing you were going for there, but I think I lost them. They don't see women as power figures. Mothers, Mistresses, Madonnas. That about covers it.

They also wonder how two people named Anthony and Carmela came up with a daughter named Meadow. But those are minor details.

"The only thing that's not real is the psychiatrist broad," said another goodfella. "But it's the movies. What are you gonna do?"

True story:

There was a young woman from the neighborhood married a wannabe wiseguy named Cuddles. Couple years go by. This and that. The next thing you know, Cuddles is a suspect in two murders and the wife's getting jammed up as an accessory.

Long story short, she thinks he's gonna kill her. She turns to the feds and becomes a cooperating witness. For a while they got her stashed in South Dakota.

"Sioux freakin' Falls, South freakin' Dakota," she tells me later. "There's more people live around Sixth and Catharine [her old neighborhood] than the whole freakin' city."

She doesn't say "freakin'" of course, which is the beauty of doing your show for HBO.

Anyway, she divorces Cuddles, testifies against him, and then, you're not gonna believe this, she marries one of the FBI agents assigned to guard her.

They move back to the area. She tells me stories about her two marriages, which sound real similar. I ask her, "What's the difference between the cops and the wiseguys?"

Without missing a beat, she goes, "The cops got badges."

True story.

I've been writing about these guys for about twenty years now and the thing that has always struck me, and the thing that many people don't realize, is that wiseguys are as multidimensional and diverse as any other group. There are doctors and lawyers and teachers who are interesting and others who aren't worth five minutes of your time. Same thing with mobsters. You capture a lot of that in the series. I once had lunch with a guy from North Jersey—could have been the prototype for Tony Soprano. His name was Michael Taccetta. We were up in Toms River where he, his brother, and two other guys were being tried on murder and racketeering charges.

Guy named Vincent Craparotta got killed in a dispute over some business deal that went sour. Craparotta, whose nickname was "Jimmy Sinatra," was beaten to death with golf clubs. An informant witness said the hitters told him they used clubs instead of baseball bats because they found in the past that "baseball bats break."

This Michael Taccetta wasn't accused of beating the guy, but was charged with setting the hit in motion. He and his brother ended up convicted of racketeering and are now doing heavy time.

One day during the trial I'm eating in the same restaurant and he invites me over to his table. First he thinks I'm a cop. Just wants to know who I am. When he finds out I'm a reporter, he invites me to join him. We have a nice conversation over chicken salad sandwiches and Cokes. He asks about some "people" from Philadelphia. He talks about his family. His kids. Whether they're going to make it in college. And he talks about the trial and about his other "problems."

He knows he's the target of a big federal investigation and figures even if he beats the murder rap, he's going to spend a lot of time in court fighting other charges. Then he takes a bite out of his sandwich and a swig from his Coke.

He looks over and he says, "It's like Willie Loman said, 'It comes with the territory.'"

First wiseguy I ever heard quoting from "Death of a Salesman."

There was another guy down here I got friendly with. We used to talk sports all the time. The guy loved the Philadelphia Eagles. He was a gambler and a bookmaker. Always flashing a big wad of cash. But when it came to the Eagles, he lost all perspective. Couldn't bring himself to bet against them, no matter what the odds or what the game situation. Cost him a fortune. Used to lay ten grand on a game.

One particular Sunday he's a wreck. "The Birds," that's how he referred to the Eagles, were playing Dallas. The game was on television. But at the same time, his six-year-old daughter had a soccer match. He didn't know where to be. A classic problem for any father. He had to choose between his obligations to work and family.

His solution was also typical. He paced the sidelines, cheering a pack of little girls who were all trying to kick a black and white ball into a net. But whenever he could, he ran over to his car, turned on the radio, and listened for an update on the football game.

"They're only young for a little while," he said of his daughter. "I hate to miss any of it."

This, of course, is the same guy who would go on an expletive-laced rant about the FBI and government informants, complaining about "lying rats," decrying the prosecution's use of witnesses whose testimony was bought and paid for, witnesses who would sell out their former friends to avoid being prosecuted for their own crimes. He's also the guy who was picked up on a tapped phone bragging about how he brutally beat a long-time associate in a dispute over money. Laughed about how he pummeled the helpless associate, a wannabe wiseguy who stood about five-foot-four and weighed close to 400 pounds.

Heartless? It sure sounded like it on the tape. Mean spirited? Any time the topic of witnesses came up. But there he was on that Sunday afternoon running up and down the sidelines watching his little girl kick a ball. He's doing fourteen years now on a racketeering conviction. Missed his daughter's

First Communion. Will probably miss her Confirmation. And a dozen birthdays and Christmases as well. Maybe even her wedding.

Is it worth it? Probably not. But it's who he is.

While we're on the subject, most of the guys say you handled the informant problem just right. They liked Big Pussy, but they saw the end coming. There was no other way. Dealing with cooperating witnesses has been a big issue down here for years. You may not know it, but South Philadelphia has more mob rats per capita than any other city in America. Long before the Sopranos, we had the South Philadelphia Boys Choir.

Omerta?

Fuhgeddaboutit. In Philadelphia it's like the Liberty Bell. Cracked and inoperative. It don't work.

Everybody talks about Sammy Gravano, but he was nothing compared to the parade of wiseguys who have given it up in federal court in Philadelphia. The best might have been Philip Leonetti. This was a kid—he was in his thirties at the time—who was considered one of the most violent hit men in the city. He grew up in Cosa Nostra. His uncle was the boss of the family. Looking back on it now, you realize he never had a chance to go in any other direction. He finally figured that out on his own and when he decided to cooperate he brought a presence to the witness stand that mesmerized and charmed jury after jury.

A defense lawyer once tried to rile him, asking questions about the various murders he was involved in. Called him ruthless. Asked, sarcastically, if he knew what ruthless meant.

"I don't think we were ruthless," Leonetti replied calmly. "We just killed people. That's what we did. That was our life."

I thought you hit that note perfectly last season.

I know there was some criticism about the wanton violence, particularly the story line about the go-go dancer who was brutally beaten to death. But to me, I saw that as your way of responding to your critics. That plot, more than any other, showed that these guys are not glamorous or noble, that their life is not about honor and loyalty. It's about money and power and greed and control.

Nobody, not Tony, not Paulie Walnuts, nobody, cared about the young dancer. And when she turned up dead, the only issue was whether anyone would get linked to the crime.

Ruthless? "It's what we do."

Leonetti was the government's star witness in the late 1980s and early 1990s. He testified at a dozen trials in seven or eight different states, includ-

ing the Toms River golf club case. Now we have Ralph Natale, a former mob boss, who became a government witness two years ago. Highest ranking made member of the Mob ever to "flip." Testified against the former mayor of Camden in a political corruption case. Then turned on his former underboss and a half dozen other guys in a big racketeering trial.

This Natale was a real piece of work. Talked a much better game than he played. But the government bought his act. He's probably going to get a "get out of jail free" card in exchange for his testimony. This despite the fact that he is a career drug trafficker and admitted murderer. Took part in a dozen Mob hits over his lifetime, including a shooting one Christmas night in which he blew two holes in the back of a friend's head. He and the victim were involved in a dispute over control of a labor union. The victim also happened to be the godfather to one of Natale's kids.

La famiglia?

Right.

We had defense attorneys digging up all kinds of dirt about Natale, who is sixty-six. It turned into a real soap opera, particularly the stuff about his relationship with a twenty-eight-year-old woman who at one time was best friends with his daughter.

Among other things, she had a tattoo done to commemorate her relationship with the Mafia don. Had the word "Natale's" scrawled just below her waistline. Next to it was an arrow pointing downward.

You can't make this stuff up.

We had an underboss, Skinny Joey Merlino, who became a local celebrity. Used to feed the homeless at Christmas time. Big party. Lots of media coverage. I say "used to" because Merlino's doing time now. Got nailed by Natale and another cooperator, Ronnie Previte. Previte, who used to be a cop, goes maybe 300 pounds.

He's on the witness stand. Merlino's at the defense table and everybody's talking about Skinny Joey and the Fat Rat.

True story:

A couple of low-life Mob associates were concerned about their business partner, a loan shark. They thought the guy was cooperating with the feds.

This goes back maybe ten, fifteen years, when Little Nicky Scarfo was the boss. Talk about a psychopath.

Anyway, these two low-lifes want to hire a hit man to kill their partner. But they don't have the money—fifteen large—to cover expenses, so to speak.

So they get this schlump from the neighborhood and they tell him to ask the loan shark if he could borrow $15,000. They tell the schlump not to worry, he won't have to pay it back. What's more, they vouch for the schlump. Tell their loan shark partner he's good for it.

The guy gets the fifteen large, gives it to the two low-lifes. They pay the hit man and the loan shark gets popped. Only time in history a guy paid for his own murder.

True story.

A personal aside. I know you're taking heat from some Italian American groups who think the show reinforces all the negative stereotypes about our heritage. I get some of the same stuff down here when I write about the real thing.

Don't let them get to you.

We know what our contributions to the world have been over generations. There's a great line in a Gay Talese magazine article from twenty years ago.

A young Italian immigrant boy in New York runs crying to his father because some of the other kids, whose parents are English and Irish and have been in the country longer, have called him a "wop."

The father hugs the boy and tells him don't cry.

"Always remember, Angelo my son, this country was discovered by one Italian, named after another Italian, and we Italians were giving art and culture to the world when the English were still living in caves and painting their faces blue."

The only people who buy into stereotypes are the weak and narrow-minded. These are people who cut their spaghetti with a knife and eat it with a spoon. Pay them no mind and don't let concerns about them stifle your creativity.

Not for nothing did Shakespeare set some of his greatest works in Italy. Whenever the Bard needed passion, pathos, humor, whenever he wanted to tell a story about the human condition, whenever he needed characters who reached out and grabbed life with all their hearts, both their hands, and any other appendage that worked, he told a story about Italians. When he wanted morose and brooding, we got Hamlet, or the Scottish play or a story about a British king. Think about it.

For too long in this country there has been a trend to turn victimization into power. This reduces accountability and throws meritocracy out the window. I worry when these Italian American groups try to claim victimhood and use it as a hammer to drive home their agenda. I understand their argument, I just don't agree with it. Maybe my grandfather and your grandfather experienced discrimination because their names ended in vowels. I look around today and I don't see it.

Tony Soprano doesn't represent me or anyone I know. He is a character in a dramatic and well-written television series. He is not an icon, not a poster boy.

The point, of course, is that neither you nor James Gandolfini see Tony Soprano in that light. I think the charm of the character—and I know "charm" may be a stretch given the context of the stories—is that Tony Soprano is Everyman, dealing with the complex problems of life in ways that don't always seem logical or make sense. But then, don't we all? The appeal is that this is Everyman played against the backdrop of organized crime. Anti-Italian? Hardly. It's classic drama.

Those who don't like the show can whine and complain and write letters to Congress. Or they can change the channel.

Sure, there are people who don't like us because we're Italian Americans. And yes, there are people who think any "Eye-talian" who has succeeded must be connected. But those attitudes are so blatantly racist and unintelligent that they hardly require a response.

To advocate any form of censorship in response to that kind of thinking is absurd. Thomas Jefferson said it best: "Freedom of expression cannot be limited without being lost."

True story:

Couple of wiseguys have just whacked a guy in South Philadelphia and they're gonna take the body over to Jersey to dump it. They put the corpse in the trunk of their car and head for the Walt Whitman Bridge.

They get in the exact change lane. This is when the bridge fare was 75 cents each way. They're in line. Cars in front. Cars in back. Then they look at one another.

Neither guy's got any change.

They got a body in the trunk. They're jammed in traffic and they don't have any coins. Now they got to maneuver out of the lane. Car horns honking. Drivers screaming.

One of the guys jumps out of the car. Stops traffic in another lane. Waves his partner in. Jumps back in the car. They hand the toll taker a dollar bill. Get a quarter in change and head over the bridge to dump the body.

True story.

Anyway, all the best for the new season. The guys down here will be watching.

And if you'd like to use any of the above for next season, give me a call.

We'll do lunch.

I know a nice joint downtown.

Great ziti.

The Mafia of Mario Puzo is no more. The noble men of honor, if they existed at all, disappeared two generations ago with the death of Carlo Gambino in New York and the assassination of Angelo Bruno in Philadelphia. They were the prototypes for Don Corleone. Men like Gambino and Bruno, in another time and in another place, could have been the CEOs of major corporations. They were that smart, that intelligent. They came to this country, struggled as immigrants, found their opportunities limited, and chose organized crime as a way of life. The choice is not one that should be applauded, but given the circumstances in which they found themselves as young men, it is at least understandable.

Today the best and the brightest in the Italian American communities of this country are doctors and lawyers, teachers and actors, engineers and scientists. And the ranks of the Mob are filled by those who are too lazy or too ignorant to know any better.

"Goodfellas?" said a lawyer, watching one of the last racketeering trials unfold in Philadelphia. "These are Dumbfellas."

"They're scraping the bottom of the gene pool," said another as he compared the mobsters of the 1990s to those of the 1950s.

Angelo Bruno was the boss of the Philadelphia mob from 1959 until his murder in 1980. He lived in a row home, wore suits bought off the rack, drove a Buick, and had a "job" as a commission salesman for a vending machine company. Over the course of his career, he spent less than three years in jail. When he died, he was a millionaire with land holdings in Florida, a stock portfolio, and investments in legitimate business. He believed in making money, not making headlines. Of the six bosses who have run the Philadelphia Mob since Bruno, one was killed and five are in jail. A series of federal racketeering prosecutions has dismantled the organization, reducing it to little more than a street corner gang.

In New York, the five families are still functioning, but hardly at the level of efficiency that typified Gambino's era. Instead, the organizations have been dominated by a celebrity gangster who is now dying in jail—John Gotti—and by a reclusive Mafia don—Vincent Gigante—who avoided prosecution for years by pretending to be crazy. Men of honor? I don't think so.

Both were done in by the testimony of Mob informants, another phenomenon of the current generation. For old-timers like Gambino and Bruno, the Mafia truly was a way of life. For the next generation, for a guy like Gotti in New York or Nicky Scarfo in Philadelphia, the Mafia was a way to make money. And those they brought into their organizations realized that immediately. Consequently, when they found themselves jammed up and facing a potential life sentence in a racketeering case, they didn't think about omerta, they thought about business. You can almost see Sammy the Bull Gravano sitting in prison calculating, "How do I cut my losses?" The answer: become a cooperating witness. It's the smart move.

The Sopranos accurately captures the turmoil and disorganization that have brought about the demise of the American Mafia. The reasons, cultural and generational, are clearly a part of the story line. Tony's struggle to keep things running smoothly, his references to the old days when things were better, and his frustration in dealing with young mobsters like his nephew or the son of his former Mob boss could come right from the transcripts of court testimony I have heard or secretly recorded conversations I have listened to.

Mario Puzo's Mafia was noble and honorable, albeit drenched in blood. David Chase's Mafia is more Americanized and less honorable, but just as bloody. Both reflect, with a nod toward dramatic and artistic license, a small piece of the Italian American experience. But they are not who we are.

There is an article that appeared in the *New York Post* a few years ago that I clipped and keep hanging on a bulletin board near my desk. It is written, I assume, partly with tongue in cheek. The headline reads "Shakespeare: A paisan?" The story is about an Italian professor who believes that the Bard was actually born Michelangelo Florio Crollalanza and that he and his parents fled Italy to avoid the Inquisition. They were Calvinists. Crollalanza eventually made his way to England, where his mother's cousins lived. They had already changed their name to Shakespeare. They had a son, William, who had died as a child. Michelangelo Crollalanza took his dead cousin's name after the family took him in. Nice story. Probably not true. But the best part was this: The professor contends that his research shows that Shakespeare was born in Messina.

Shakespeare, then, was not only Italian, but Sicilian. It would explain a lot.

I have another excerpt hanging near my desk that comes from an article that appeared in *Life* magazine in 1939. It was a profile of Joe DiMaggio. I keep it to remind me of how far we have come and how times have changed. The piece reads in part: "Although he learned Italian first, Joe, now 24, speaks English without an accent, and is otherwise well adapted to most U.S. mores. Instead of olive oil or smelly bear grease he keeps his hair slick with water. He never reeks of garlic and prefers chicken chow mein to spaghetti."[1]

DiMaggio, Sinatra, La Guardia, they had to deal with that nonsense. Show me where or when they whined or complained. Their answer was to be the best—the absolute best—at what they did. DiMaggio's fifty-six-game hitting streak is perhaps the one baseball record that will never be broken. Sinatra's ability to interpret a lyric cannot be matched. La Guardia's political sympatico was unparalleled. In their own way, each set the standard by which others are now measured. DiMaggio had that quiet class and style. Sinatra the confident swagger. La Guardia the uncanny ability to connect with the people he served. They set the bar. Centuries ago the Romans coined a phrase that described it best. "Sine qua non," they said.

Finally, there is this story, told to me by my father-in-law whose father, like DiMaggio's father and my grandfather, came to America from Sicily in the early 1900s.

My father-in-law's father—my wife's grandfather—arrived in a small town in Southern New Jersey and went to work as a migrant laborer on a farm just outside of Swedesboro. Every night the owner of the farm, a German American, would lock my wife's grandfather and grandmother in the attic on the third floor of his farmhouse. This was because, as everyone knew, Sicilians were dangerous and untrustworthy and carried knives with which they could slit your throat. So every night during that hot, South Jersey summer, they were locked in a stuffy attic. Each morning they were allowed out to work the fields.

Welcome to America.

Time passed. My father-in-law's father settled in the town of Swedesboro. He and his wife raised a family. Two of their sons, my father-in-law and his brother, went off to fight in World War II. Every month they would send money home to "Pop," money he was to save for them because they were engaged and hoped to marry once the war was over. Both brothers survived and returned home. And when they asked their father about the money, he told them to get in his truck and he took them for a ride.

They rode a short distance outside of town to an old farmhouse, the farmhouse where he had been locked in the attic so many years before. And he said to his sons, "There's your money." He had bought the farm. It is where my wife and her brothers and her cousin were born and raised.

I never knew my wife's grandfather. He had passed away before she and I met. But my father-in-law tells that story with great pride. I think of the old man driving out to that farm with his sons. I think of how proud he must have been of them and of his own ability to buy that property for them. I think of how he must have felt as he watched his grandchildren grow up on that farm and of how he would feel now if he could see those grandchildren and their children with college degrees and careers and a piece of the American dream he came looking for so many years ago.

He was locked in an attic because he was Italian. He was distrusted and feared not because of anything he had done, but because of what someone else thought of him. He didn't whine. He didn't complain. He had too much pride for that. He went about his business. He built a better life for himself and for his family. And in the end, in a move so typically Sicilian, he had the last word.

He knew who he was.

CONTRIBUTORS

GEORGE ANASTASIA, a reporter for the *Philadelphia Inquirer*, has written about organized crime for the past twenty years. He has published several books on the Mob, including *Blood and Honor*, which Jimmy Breslin called "the best gangster book ever written." Anastasia's other books are *Mob Father, The Goodfella Tapes, The Summer Wind*, and a novella, *The Big Hustle*. He has also written screenplays based on *Blood and Honor* and *The Big Hustle*. The recipient of numerous journalism awards for writing and reporting, Anastasia is a 1969 graduate of Dartmouth College with a degree in French Literature. He has also studied at the University of Florida and Swarthmore College and has been an adjunct professor/lecturer at Glassboro State College (now Rowan University) and Temple University.

REGINA BARRECA is a University of Connecticut English professor and author of the best-selling book *They Used to Call Me Snow White . . . But I Drifted, Perfect Husbands (& Other Fairy Tales), Sweet Revenge*, and *Too Much of a Good Thing Is Wonderful*. She writes a weekly column for *The Hartford Courant*, and is also the editor of *The Penguin Book of Women's Humor, Sex and Death in Victorian Literature, The Erotics of Instruction*, and the forthcoming *Don't Tell Mama: The Penguin Book of Italian American Writing*. She grew up on Ocean Avenue and Avenue T in Brooklyn, then lived in Oceanside, Long Island. Four years at Dartmouth College were followed by a Reynold's Fellowship at Cambridge University, after which she remembered where she came from and hit West 42nd Street, receiving her PhD in 1987 from The City University of New York. She lives with her husband, Michael Meyer, in Connecticut.

MICHAEL FLAMINI is an editor and writer who lives in New York City. His grandfathers, Fortunato Flamini and Giuseppi DiJinio, emigrated to the

United States from Rome in the early part of the twentieth century. His grandmothers, Rose Flamini and Rose Russell (Rosselli before immigration officials Anglicized it upon her parents' arrival in the United States), were born in the United States, but of Roman ancestry. He made his First Holy Communion at Sacred Heart Roman Catholic Church in Mahanoy City, Pennsylvania.

FRED GARDAPHÉ directs the American and Italian/American Studies Programs at the State University of New York at Stony Brook. He is Associate Editor of *Fra Noi,* editor of the Series in Italian American Culture at the State University of New York Press, and co-founding co-editor of *Voices in Italian Americana,* a literary journal and cultural review. He is also past President of the American Italian Historical Association (1996–2000). His books include *Italian Signs, American Streets: The Evolution of Italian American Narrative, Dagoes Read: Tradition and the Italian/American Writer,* and *Moustache Pete Is Dead!: Italian/American Oral Tradition Preserved in Print.* His edited books include *New Chicago Stories, Italian American Ways,* and *From the Margin: Writings in Italian Americana.* He has written two one-act plays: "Vinegar and Oil," produced by the Italian/American Theatre Company in 1987, and "Imported from Italy," produced by Zebra Crossing Theater in 1991. He recently finished a book entitled: *Leaving Little Italy: Essays in Italian American Studies,* and is at work on a memoir and a study of the gangster figure in American culture.

SANDRA M(ORTOLA) GILBERT, a Professor of English at the University of California, Davis, has published six collections of poetry, including, most recently, *Ghost Volcano* (1995) and *Kissing the Bread: New and Selected Poems, 1969–1999* (2000), as well as a memoir, *Wrongful Death* (1995). In addition, she has authored or co-authored numerous works of criticism, among them *Acts of Attention: The Poems of D. H. Lawrence* (1972, 1990) and (with Susan Gubar) *The Madwoman in the Attic: The Woman Writer and the 19th-Century Literary Tradition* (1979). She has also edited or co-edited many anthologies, most recently *Inventions of Farewell: A Book of Elegies* (2001). She writes often, and passionately, on Italian American topics.

JAY PARINI is a poet, novelist, and biographer. He is Axinn Professor of English at Middlebury College, where he directs the writing program. His books of poetry include *Anthracite Country* and *House of Days*. His most recent novels are *The Last Station, Benjamin's Crossing,* and *The Apprentice Lover.* He has published biographies of John Steinbeck and Robert Frost. He is also a frequent contributor to many periodicals, including the *New York Times, Harper's,* and *The Chronicle of Higher Education.*

CARLA GARDINA PESTANA is Associate Professor of History at Ohio State University, where she teaches early American history and religion, among other topics. She is a contributor to *The British Atlantic World, 1500–1800,* edited by Michael Braddick and David Armitage (Palgrave, 2002), and her book *The English Atlantic in an Era of Revolution, 1640–1661* will be published by Harvard University Press in 2004. Her Italian ancestors migrated to the United States in the last quarter of the nineteenth century. Most came from southern Italy, Napoli, and Basilacata, but family lore has her great-grandfather Gardini originating in Padova. She grew up in Southern California where she, unlike the Sopranos, knew many non-Italians.

E. ANTHONY ROTUNDO is the author of *American Manhood: Transformations in Masculinity from the Revolution to the Modern Era* (Perseus Press). He has written numerous articles on gender, family, education, and popular culture for scholarly journals and popular periodicals. He works as Instructor of History and Social Sciences at Phillips Academy in Andover, Massachusetts. His father's parents both came to America from a small village in the hills of Potenza, settling in Schenectady, New York, where they raised Rotundo in an Italian American neighborhood that no longer exists.

NOTES

CHAPTER 1: LIFE WITH (GOD)FATHER

1. See Fetterley, *The Resisting Reader: A Feminist Approach to American Fiction* (Bloomington and London: Indiana University Press, 1978).
2. Mark Armstrong, "Italian-American Lawyers Snub 'Sopranos,'" http://www.eonline.com, April 5, 2001.
3. George de Stefano, "Ungood Fellas," *The Nation* (February 7, 2000). De Stefano's own answer to the question posed by the flurry of protests and lawsuits surrounding *The Sopranos* (does "the persistence of the Mafioso as a pop-culture archetype constitute ethnic defamation of Italian-Americans?") was unequivocal: "it is dismaying—no, infuriating—to see one's group depicted so consistently in such distorted fashion."
4. Millman, "We are family: You don't have to be Italian for 'The Sopranos' to hit home," http://www.salon.com/ent/col/mill/2000/01/14.
5. James, "'The Sopranos' New Season: Blood, Bullets and Proust," *New York Times* (March 2, 2001).
6. Lavery, "Coming Heavy," http://www.poppolitics.com.
7. Alfano, "For Want of a Nail," Anti Bias Committee of UNICO National (August 25, 2001), http://community.nj.com/cc/AntiBiasCommitteeUNICONational.

CHAPTER 2:
WHY I LIKE THE WOMEN IN *THE SOPRANOS*
EVEN THOUGH I'M NOT SUPPOSED TO

1. Simone de Beauvoir, *The Second Sex*, trans. H. M. Parshley (Hamondsworth, Middlesex, England: Penguin, 1977), p. 407.

CHAPTER 3: WONDERBREAD AND STUGOTS:
ITALIAN AMERICAN MANHOOD AND *THE SOPRANOS*

1. J. G. Peristiany, "Introduction," in J. G. Peristiany, *Honour and Shame: The Values of Mediterranean Society* (Chicago: University of Chicago Press, 1966), p. 11.

2. Humbert Nelli, *From Immigrants to Ethnics: The Italian Americans* (New York: Oxford University Press, 1983), pp. 132–143; Leonard Covello, *The Social Background of the Italo-American School Child,* Francesco Cordasco, ed. (Leiden, Netherlands: E. J. Brill, 1967).

3. Donna R. Gabbacia, *From Sicily to Elizabeth Street: Housing and Social Change Among Italian Immigrants, 1880–1930* (Albany, N.Y.: State University of New York Press, 1984).

4. Jerry Mangione, *Mount Allegro: A Memoir of Italian American Life* (New York: Columbia University Press, 1981), p. 80.

5. Mangione, p. 81.

CHAPTER 5:
FRESH GARBAGE:
THE GANGSTER AS SUBURBAN TRICKSTER

1. Don DeLillo, *Underworld* (New York: Scribner, 1997), p. 277.
2. Ibid., p. 287.
3. Wallace Katz, "Sticking Together, Falling Apart: The Sopranos and the American Moral Order." *New Labor Forum* (Fall/Winter 2001): p. 95.
4. Ibid., p. 93.
5. Ibid., p. 95.
6. Eric Lott, *Love and Theft: Blackface Minstrelsy and the American Working Class* (New York: Oxford University Press, 1995), p. 25.
7. Ibid., pp. 25–26; p. 52.
8. Cited in Lott, p. 149.
9. David Ruth, *Inventing the Public Enemy: The Gangster in American Culture, 1918–1934* (Chicago: University of Chicago Press, 1996), p. 3.
10. Jonathan Munby, *Public Enemies, Public Heroes* (Chicago: University of Chicago Press, 1999), p. 2.
11. Ibid., p. 4.
12. Jack Shadoian, *Dreams and Dead Ends: The American Gangster/Crime Film* (Cambridge, MA: MIT University Press, 1977), p. 4.
13. Ibid., p. 5.
14. Gaetano Cipolla, *What Makes a Sicilian?* (Brooklyn, NY: Legas, 1996), p. 16.
15. Robert Fishman, *Bourgeois Utopias: The Rise and Fall of Suburbia* (New York: Basic Books, 1987), p. 190.
16. Ibid., p. 6.
17. Ibid., p. x.
18. Ibid., p. 38.
19. Cited in Kenneth T. Jackson, *Crabgrass Frontier: The Suburbanization of the United States* (New York: Oxford University Press, 1985), p. 62.
20. Michael Klein, "Beyond the American Dream: Film and the Experience of a Defeat." In *An American Half-Century: Postwar Culture and the Politics in the*

USA. Ed. Michael Klein (London and Boulder, CO: Pluto Press, 1994), p. 221.

21. Richard Vetere, *Gangster Apparel* (Woodstock, IL: Dramatic Publishing, 1996); revised 2001. This quote has been added to the third act of the revised play, which is not yet published.

22. Ibid.

23. Stanley Diamond, "Introductory Essay: Job and the Trickster." In Paul Radin, *The Trickster* (New York: Schocken Books, 1956), p. xiii.

24. Ibid., p. xxi.

25. Paul Radin, *The Trickster* (New York: Schocken Books, 1956), p. xxiv.

26. C. G. Jung, "On the Psychology of the Trickster Figure." In Paul Radin, *The Trickster* (New York: Schocken Books, 1956), p. 201.

27. Ibid., p. 207.

28. Ibid., p. 207.

CHAPTER 6:
"PA CENT' ANNI, DR. MELFI"

1. Monica McGoldrick, Joe Giordano, and John Pearce, eds. *Ethnicity and Family Therapy* (2nd ed., New York: Guilford Press, 1996), p. 567.

2. Joseph Ponterotto, et al., *Cultural Diversity and Ethnic Minority Psychology* (Washington, D.C.: Educational Foundation Publishing, 2001), pp. 362–375.

3. Ibid.

CHAPTER 7:
CATHOLICISM, IDENTITY, AND ETHICS IN *THE SOPRANOS*

1. I would like to thank Don, my viewing companion and *consigliere,* for help with this essay.

2. He describes his parents as Baptist and "socialist atheist"; see Alex Witchel, *The Son Who Created a Hit,* The Sopranos. *The New York Times on* The Sopranos (New York: Ibooks, 2000): p. 46.

3. Robin Dougherty, "Chasing TV" (interview with David Chase), http://www.salon.com/ent/int/1999/01/20int.html.

4. U.S. Census Bureau, *Statistical abstract of the United States* (Section 1, Population) (Washington, D.C.: G.P.O., 2000), p. 61. The number of Baptists would be higher, except that they are divided into numerous denominations.

5. They are identified as "Russian thugs" in Allen Rucker, *The Sopranos: A Family History* (Rev. ed., New York: Penguin, Putnam Inc., 2001), season one synopsis, n.p.

6. Robert Anthony Orsi, *The Madonna of 115th Street: Faith and Community in Italian Harlem, 1880–1950* (New Haven: Yale University Press, 1985), pp. 204–207.

7. Gallop poll results summarized in Dave Condren, "Book Helps Family, Friends Deal with Pain when a Catholic Leaves the Faith," *Buffalo News* (May 12, 2001, final ed.).

8. HBO website, http://www.hbo.com.

9. John Paul II, "Heaven, Hell and Purgatory" (July 1999), http://www.ewtn.com/library/PAPALCOC/JP2 HEAVEN.HTM, p. 6.

CHAPTER 8:
IF SHAKESPEARE WERE ALIVE TODAY,
HE'D BE WRITING FOR *THE SOPRANOS*

1. *Life* (May 1, 1939).

INDEX